The B2B Sales Top Tips Guidebook

Jim Irving – supported by his friends – now delivers his third book. The first two were highly successful, and award winning. He has created a piece of work which uniquely delivers serious focus onto 36 individual skills, challenges, techniques, and ideas to help you sell B2B better. World leading advice from experts, coaches, authors, thought leaders, B2B buyers and many others – with each one having lived, experienced and excelled in their chosen subject. True wisdom from the best!

"Experience is a cruel teacher. It gives a test before presenting the lesson."
Anonymous

1

The B2B Sales Top Tips Guidebook
First edition - 2021 by Jim Irving, distributed
in partnership with ebookpartnership.com
Copyright © Jim Irving 2021.
(Note: all of the content within guest chapters
remains the copyright of those individuals)

ISBN 9798758258248

This book is available in e-book and
paperback formats.

Layout by Alan Davison at HERO-Creative.com

Partner

noun \ *pärt-nər*

A person who shares or is associated with another in some action or endeavor; associate...

Source: Random House Websters Dictionary

 Jim was born in Edinburgh, Scotland and now lives in rural Northern Ireland with his wife, Yvonne. He spent over 30 years in corporate Business to Business (B2B) selling and business leadership roles in a number of tier one technology organisations including Amdahl, Sequent, Silicon Graphics (SGI) and Information Builders (www.ibi.com).

Over the last 15 years, since leaving the corporate world and starting his own consultancy, he has improved the sales processes and results and mentored the business leaders in many early stage and SME (Small to Medium Enterprise) organisations.

His career started with the hardest possible assignment – selling office equipment door to door in Scotland, in the depths of winter! His career rapidly developed into senior selling and sales leadership roles then ultimately to senior executive positions at major multinationals – including becoming the UK MD of Information Builders – a leading US based enterprise software company. At Silicon Graphics he was awarded the Corporation's 'Exemplary Leader' award. Jim has also held several executive marketing leadership posts. In recent years Jim has been both the Managing Director of an SME tech company and VP of sales and marketing for another.

Jim has travelled extensively and worked in over 25 countries worldwide. He gained an MBA from Edinburgh Napier University in 1988. He is a Fellow of both the Chartered Institute of Marketing and The Institute of Sales Professionals. He has spoken at a number of seminars and conferences and has in the past been an occasional visiting lecturer to the Postgraduate Business schools at two leading UK universities.

His first two books have become award winning, highly rated publications. Supporting comments from leading sales authors, positive reviews from The Institute of Sales Management and The Chartered Institute of Marketing, plus winning a 'Best Sales Books of 2021' Award from 'BookAuthority' position him as both an excellent author and thought leader in this space. Consistent 5* Amazon reviews have further cemented his reputation.

When not working, Jim enjoys dining out, family time, walking in the country, travel, reading fiction and following current affairs.

Some Comments on Jim's work

"Pick up a copy of this amazing enterprise selling book and break out the highlighters!!" I have just finished reading 'The B2B Selling Guidebook' by author Jim Irving. It is clear Jim is a big-time money-ball seller. His enterprise selling stories and business cases are moving and motivating. It is clear author Irving wants to leave something personal for the business community. His ideas are crystal clear and worth repeating. Pick up a copy and break out the highlighters!"

Patrick Tinney, world famous author of 'Perpetual Hunger', 'Unlocking Yes' and 'The Bonus Round'.

"Complete with an exclamation mark, 'keep learning' are the final two words of this excellent book by Jim Irving. Like a stick of Margate or Blackpool rock, those two words are weaved through all twenty-one chapters. Aimed at seasoned salespeople as well as novices, this little black book is a cornucopia of sales content and personal anecdotes from Jim's forty plus years in sales. The entire book is written in Plain English (a pleasant change) and there are some excellent appendices at the back. I'm reading this book again I liked it so much."

Jeremy Jacobs, The Sales Rainmaker

"Mentorship is something I've embraced this year with the brilliant Jim Irving. Having spent decades working in business and published multiple books on the topic, Jim's wealth of knowledge and expertise was the sort of influence I didn't realise was missing from my life. He has become an invaluable friend to me as I seek to follow in his career footsteps, and with his guidance, I'm slowly but surely beginning to trust that I actually do know what I'm doing, even if it doesn't feel like it. His mentorship at this stage of my career has been indispensable..."

Adam Cree, Chief Revenue Officer, 3EN

For my Sister, Irene

Preface

*"Alone we can do so little;
together we can do so much."*

Helen Keller

My first book, 'The B2B Selling Guidebook', sold better than I had expected. It went on to gather consistent 5* reviews. It was then awarded a world-wide 'Best Sales Books of 2021" placing. This was a big award and very unexpected for a first-time author.

The follow up was aimed at a much smaller audience than that first 'universe' of salespeople. The B2B Leaders Guidebook (for sales team and small business leaders) also gathered great reviews, plus recommendations from professional bodies and readers alike. However, the very act of writing two books in quick succession proved to be a hard, demanding, and time-consuming task.

After a short gap I mentioned to my wife, Yvonne, about my idea of writing yet another one! No sooner had the words left my mouth than she replied. *"Tell you what, I have an idea for the title."* Intrigued, I asked her what it was. Without a second's hesitation she said *"The B2B Divorce Guidebook!".*

And here it is! But with a different title - thankfully. 😄 After a while, I was given leave to write this one, but only on the condition that it was definitely the last. And it will be.

My first book was full to the brim of my tips and ideas on B2B Sales. The second was based on my many years of leadership and management, again it focussed entirely on my own experience and ideas.

So, what should I do in creating the third book?

Around the time I was sitting, trying to gain inspiration for the book, (with a blank sheet of paper in front of me), I coincidentally decided to run a little competition on LinkedIn (I am a very regular 'poster' and contributor). I asked those who connected with me or followed my work just to tell me about their top tip on selling. I was inundated! After I had decided on the winners and then sent out their prizes, I suddenly realised just how great all the submissions had been. I started to call round fellow authors, thought leaders, famous speakers, high level business retirees, salespeople, procurement professionals and business owners (who have to deal with B2B salespeople!) and others who just had a great story or idea.

Before I knew it, I had 26 guest articles from the sales, buying, business and personal perspectives. All different, all unique, each packed with insight, experience and value. That's why the first print page of the book references 'partner'. These people are my friends, my business contacts and each is a great example to me. Together we have partnered to deliver something that I believe is both unique and very special. I have also added another 10 chapters of my own. New insights from me that build on my first two books.

Writing this book was a very different exercise. Instead of me slogging away every day, I had to wait, to see what came back, from each individual. A very different experience and, yes, 'herding cats' did come to mind a few times!

I am very proud of this book and so thankful to my good friends from around the world who have helped me to create it. Contributions have come in from the USA, Canada, Australia, the UK and Europe. Each different and special. The fact that they each took some time out of their busy lives to write a chapter for me has been inspiring and a wonderful experience for me. These individuals are true partners – working to help me bring something different to the world of B2B sales. What started with a little 'lightbulb' moment is now what you hold in your hands. Thanks only to my guest authors.

The guest chapters are written from each author's experience of one challenge, attribute, approach, or skill. I would guess that, if all were put in a room together, there might be disagreements about the best ways to do things. Who knows, you might disagree with any one of my own, or my guest's, chapters! BUT, as a body, this book represents something over 740 years of sales experience distilled into 36 short chapters. Yes, 740+ years...

I want you to enjoy the book, take time to think, but most of all learn from this unrivalled body of experience. Ignoring real-world experience is not a clever approach most of the time. All the contributors to the book have learned these tips, often the hard way. Let us now help you. The book covers a very broad range of topics. Dig in and enjoy!

Jim Irving
Northern Ireland, November 2021

"Working together is success..."

Henry Ford

Also available from Jim Irving...

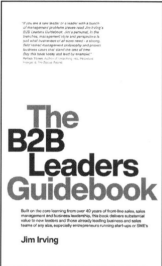

Contents

Introduction

Chapter

1

Consistency – the True Breakfast of Champions!

By Jim Irving

"Success isn't always about 'greatness'. It's about consistency. Consistent hard work gains success. Greatness will come."

Dwayne Johnson

Some things are just SO underrated. Wearing good quality shoes. Smiling. Enjoying the sun on your face (trust me, in Northern Ireland that's something I look forward to 😎). And consistency...

And here I mean the good type of breakfast of champions – not the 'ironic' beer, pizza or whatever. I am thinking more of muesli, Weetabix (UK) or Wheaties (US and Canada)!

In researching this article, I looked up google.
"The importance of consistency in business" resulted in 176 million articles – hmmm, I think my hunch was confirmed just by that alone.

Interestingly, changing the search from 'business' to 'branding' also yielded many millions of hits too.

Consistency is boring. Absolutely. But so are really good shoes. I have several pairs of Loake's (www.loake.com) that are now around 20 years old. They fit like gloves, they have never let me down, they still look good. Multiple changes of soles of course, but the core is still the same. What have they delivered to me? Long term use, reliability, serious quality and... consistency. I know exactly what I am getting. And that's the thing, isn't it? As individual buyers that's what we are looking for. It's the same with business procurement AND in our own sales journey.

Think for a moment about a strong brand. You know the colour, perhaps the strapline, what it stands for, maybe their jingle. It means something. Of course, we all have our own personal brand. If we do nothing about it, it just sits there, it's just 'me'. But is it consistent? Would those you meet in business all say the same about you? Would they compare notes and see the same attributes or strengths? In my experience dealing with professional salespeople, the answer is often no. And that is a weakness.

While its boring, consistency leads to both trust and success...

You can view consistency in two ways. Inward/internal and outwards.

Internal consistency.

How can you deliver great service and service levels if you aren't consistent? It's the bedrock of all you do.

Make sure you deliver every time, not some of the time. Ensure that what you do is both focussed and aligned to your company direction and goals.

Build your own brand. What do you stand for? How do you work? What sets you apart? Then stick to it and just 'be it' in all your selling ventures. People like and are attracted by this form of consistency. Live up to everything you commit to.

Finally, take time to analyse and reflect. How are you doing in your role? Is your performance good enough? Are your values shining through? Trust me, people notice. In fact, once you set your own levels people develop an expectation for you and your performance and behaviour. A few times I have fallen far short of what I want to be. Almost immediately those I was engaged with expressed surprise and disappointment. Because of my internal standards they had trust and faith – and I let them down. But the flip side is that having that faith made them great customers and friends, who thankfully forgave me...

External consistency.

Being consistent does wonders for your reputation and status in your marketplace. You build trust, you are seen as reliable, gaining access becomes easier over time. Again, it's boring, but not everything good is exciting!

Being consistent as you reach out to prospects is also powerful. Think of some leading examples like Apple, BMW and Coca-Cola. Everyone knows what they do, how they function, what sets them apart. Consistency breeds loyalty. One of the most successful long-term messaging and ad campaigns in the UK is for a brand of wood stains, Ronseal. It has become their logo and a phrase that is now used in common conversation – *"It does exactly what it says on the tin".* How boring is that, but how effective! They are saying, if you buy from us, you will get precisely what is pictured and said on the tin you purchase. Of course, the magic only happens with good execution. I use their products and they do! Now you have a virtuous circle. You sell better because you just do what you say you will. There is a big lesson there for everyone in sales.

When you are consistent, you can manage and focus your team, your resources, and your strengths much more easily. In fact, several business gurus suggest that consistency is the true secret sauce that leads to real greatness.

Consistency delivers three powerful returns -

1. **Relevance.** The more consistent you are, the more known and relevant you become to your prospects. That in turn creates a feeling of trust and certainty in them.
2. **Clarity.** Rather than spending time and energy re-inventing and changing everything, find your consistent process, attitude, and approach – and stick to them! Clarity makes everything easier for you.
3. **Accountability.** This is a positive thing in case you were wondering! Quality control is about consistency. Formalised sales pipeline processes are about consistency. Departments working together and delivering success are about consistency.

One of the biggest outputs from consistency is the concept of the 'replicable process'. By this I mean the following...

You move into a new role. You know nothing, so you learn from others, then you start to head out and meet prospects. Maybe things go well, but more frequently you hit bumps along your road. After a while you figure out what really works for you. Things start to gel. Most frequently, what you have just done is to find a 'replicable process' – that set of steps, questions, actions that result in the right things happening for you. A replicable process is another output from consistency – and it is also a real-world manifestation of consistency.

The lesson. Think of those people you have met who are seriously unpredictable. They can be fun, but also wearing. When you don't know where you stand with them, are you trusting, are you sure they will deliver? Of course not. Organisations buy based on many factors. The product or service itself, yes. References, yes. Price, yes. And on trust - based on consistency, absolutely. Finally, given a choice, buyers will always take consistency over intensity! Is your own sales process replicable? Is it successful? Does it work for you? If not, keep working till you achieve it.

Notes

Chapter

2

The Fortune is in the Follow Up

By Brittany Baldwin

"Diligent follow-up and follow-through will set you apart from the crowd and communicate excellence."

John C Maxwell

Sales success starts and finishes with you.

The unfortunate truth is that very few people aspire to be salespeople. The reason for this is because, for many years, the sales profession has been synonymous with dangerously unethical persuasive tactics.

There was a time when salespeople were schooled in the art of deceit and manipulation. They were smooth talking, cheap suit wearing, vacuum demonstrating individuals who overpromised and underdelivered.

Salespeople no longer operate this way and evolution has largely weeded out these traditional sales techniques, yet the stigma still remains.

The modern approach to selling is one where salespeople are professional communicators. They listen to their customer, identify their needs, and help them solve their problems.

So, the bottom line is this. You need to reframe your thinking and shift your mindset around selling.

Accept the fact that sales is an honest profession and, once you can confidently sell to yourself then you can unlock your potential to start selling to others.

Depending on which study you believe, it takes an average of 8 contacts with a customer before they're ready to buy from you. The statistics report that only 10% of salespeople follow up more than three times and 48% never follow up at all.

This proves there is a huge disconnect between the customer's buying behaviour and the majority of salespeople's effort to convert the sale.

So, here's the truth. You could have an endless list of prospects and customers, give the best presentations and have the greatest closing techniques, but if you don't follow up, you won't sign anybody up.

Follow up involves staying connected with prospects and customers with the aim of nurturing long-term relationships. It demonstrates your commitment to the customer's journey, it gives you insight into their decision making and, above all else, follow up increases opportunities to do more business with customers beyond the first sale.

Business revenue only comes from two sources: new customers and existing customers.

Whilst the modern definition of sales is all about relationship building, the aim of the sales game will always be to get prospects to buy and then to buy again.

Acquiring a new customer is at least 5 times more expensive than retaining an existing one. This is because you don't have to spend resources to go out and find a new client if you can keep your existing ones happy.

Make sense? Of course. But just because its common sense doesn't mean its common practice.

Unfortunately, business leaders and salespeople are neglecting the current opportunities and the lifetime value of customers. They are so obsessed with lead generation that they forget about their existing prospects and customers.

So instead of employing paid advertising, SEO Rankings, marketing strategies and social media posting to generate new leads, how about you look after the customers you already have in your database.

These are your warm leads. They know who you are and what you have to offer. So, take care of them or they will find another supplier who does it better than you.

Frequent and recent following up is best demonstrated through the concept of nurturing the little fish.

The saying goes "there are plenty of fish in the sea". From a sales perspective, this means there are plenty of customers in the world who could be a good fit for your product or service.

Most business leaders adopt a strategy of hunting the big whale. Their goal is to hook the major customers with deep pockets that will generate the most revenue. This is a risky business approach because, if they lose the whale, they lose a huge fraction of their revenue.

Chances are they will end up with empty lines and empty pockets.

You should consider that there is an abundance of little fish in the ocean.

Instead of devoting all your attention to whales, you should bait your hook and drip feed the little fish. They will grow attached to you and won't want to be hooked by anyone else. And in the process of supporting the little fish, eventually they will grow into big fish.

Your initial success will lead you to grow confident in your fishing abilities and you can then more effectively and successfully target the whales down the track.

As a salesperson, your intention should be to focus on retention and conversion rather than acquisition. Instead of overlooking the customers in your database in favour of new leads, reconnect with them. Build the relationship, learn more about where they're at, see if you're a good fit and then ask them to do even more business with you.

Based in Australia, **Brittany Baldwin** has a simple philosophy. She aspires to inspire before she expires.

This woman on a mission is spreading the message that selling is simple. Brittany encourages business leaders to think about the concept of time and sales as a collective so you can be in the business where you get business all the time.

Most probably just like you, Brittany is not a natural born salesperson. In fact, when she entered her first sales role, the closest Brittany had come to selling was a pair of shoes on eBay.

A little training and a whole lot of action led to Brittany's rise and rise in the sales world, earning a place as an executive within a multi-million dollar corporation, all by the age of 27. With sales records in excess of $115 million over just three years, sales is Brittany's second language.

She worked hard, sure. But her success didn't just come from working hard. It came from learning a series of simple, easy to implement steps and repeating them.

Notes

Chapter

3

Be Present in Your Deals

By Joe Barhoum

"Being fully present is the best guarantee for a bright future."

Guy Finley

One cloudy afternoon, I received a feverish phone call from a CEO whom I was advising. His tone was a mix of frustration and anger. He had a, roughly, quarter-million-dollar deal he was trying to close, and he was seeking my professional advice.

Great. That is what I was there for.

He operated a startup with tremendous growth opportunity. But he and his team were yet to have identified their ideal customer profile. Thus, every deal mattered and transactions larger than $10,000 USD were few and far between. His situation was one I had been in myself, numerous times: the buyer had "gone dark". The buyer was seeking a solution my client could provide. The problem was, the CEO desperately needed to win the deal to solve some cashflow challenges and revenue goals.

In other words: they were the solution to each other's problem.

My client could not come up with an action. He had emailed the buyer a few times in the days preceding our conversation. So, he was frustrated to have been ignored, after the buyer indicated they wanted to move forward with the transaction.

This is understandable. Why would a buyer go "dark" at this point in the cycle?

After my client expressed his emotions and asked me for help, I simply asked, *"when is the last time you called him?"*. A meaningful silence followed. I could hear his brain turning. He had just realized his mistake: he had relied on the past – he was not present in the sale. He swiftly hung up on me and called his prospective customer.

As it turns out, the buyer was technically "dark" but was thinking about the transaction actively and trying to settle on the decision before re-engaging my client. Something my client had left his prospect to stew on, all by himself. Fortunately, it was not too late, and the contract was signed later that evening. A quarter-million-dollar deal; my client's largest transaction at the time. A game changer.

The moral of this true story is, *be present in your deals*. Unfortunately, many sellers are afraid to pick up the phone. Perhaps because they do not want to be persistent to the point of annoying the buyer or they do not want to hear "no".

How does a seller avoid being in this position?

As part of my lectures, I train on what I call *The Four Rules of Great Sellers*. One of the rules is to Be Prepared. This rule applies perfectly here. To be prepared, a seller must qualify hard and fast, early, and often. Sales qualification refers to the practice of zeroing in on the "fit" of a prospect as a future customer. The basics of qualification include:

- Do I know if they have budget for my product or service?
- Do I know the process they have identified for their evaluation?
- Do I know who the ultimate decision maker is?
- Do I know the buyer's needs?
- Do I know the buyer's purchase and implementation timeline?

In sales, presence and qualification are inextricably linked. Incomplete qualification often backfires on a seller. Clearly, in the example of my client, the buyer was qualified but the seller did not know. And had he not called the buyer, perhaps the buyer would have found another solution, such as making no decision at all or going to a competitor who was more present. Had my client been more inquisitive throughout the cycle, he would have known the buyer had additional questions before signing a contract. The natural question that follows this is, "how do I avoid annoying the buyer?"

I am glad you asked.

The key is *compatibility*. Buyers want to feel good about their decision. You have heard this before: people buy from people they like and trust. How does a seller guarantee likeability and trust? They cannot. It is simply impossible to be liked and trusted by every buyer. What is in your control as a seller is to put yourself in the best position to be liked and trusted. And the method is *honesty*. Being honest is another rule I lecture on. A component of being honest is being yourself. Human beings have a BS meter (I will leave it to you to determine what that stands for). The stronger that meter goes off, the less trusting the buyer will be. In software, we demonstrate the software live instead of showing screenshots. Why? Because a buyer cannot trust screenshots alone. They can be doctored and manipulated to misrepresent what the software is capable of. Many software tools are available with free trials or feature-reduced versions which also builds trust. What many sellers do is adopt the traits of other salespeople they perceive as high-performing and, thus, enviable. They do it because they believe it will help them be more compatible with the buyer. They may try to be the funny seller or the buttoned-up, well-dressed seller. What they are really doing is hiding who they are. The challenge – and problem - is those traits are not inherent to that seller. Therefore, creating a dissonance between how the seller would naturally act and how they are pretending to act, based on the situation. That trips the BS meter. Just as, screenshots versus video. And this creates an opportunity for mistrust.

Be prepared, honest, and present. The deals will follow.

Professor **Joe Barhoum** has been selling software and services for more than 15 years, while also building and leading sales and marketing teams. Since 2013, he has been teaching Sales at the University of Portland, while developing the University's Personal Selling Certificate program for graduate students. He is the author of The Great Sellers Playbook, which he uses as a basis for his lectures, delivered to active and aspiring sellers around the globe. Since 2018, Joe has been advising CEOs through his consultancy, Conduit Construct.

Contact: Joe@conduitconstruct.com

Notes

_____

_____

_____

_____

_____

_____

_____

_____

_____

_____

_____

_____

_____

_____

_____

_____

_____

_____

_____

_____

Chapter

4

Activity

By Mark Blezard

"The real risk is doing nothing."

Denis Waitley

"Are you behind on your credit card bills? Good, pick up the phone and start dialling." "Is your landlord ready to evict you? Good, pick up the phone and start dialling." **Jordan Belfort, Wolf of Wall Street.**

Jordan actually said this during a sales meeting with his several hundred brokers. Yes, I know, he is the 'Marmite of sales.' You either love him or hate him. Now I'm going to contradict myself because I both love and hate him. I love the sales training he delivered. I hate the use of his exceptional skills to mis-sell to thousands of innocent folk.

However, there is one simple message in this quote. Activity! A well-known German sales trainer once said to me, *"I would take activity over skills any day,"* which got me thinking. Why do you want under-skilled people?

Finally, the penny dropped. What use are skills if you don't put them into practice? Sure, he wants the ideal combination of an active, skilled executive, but never with the skills alone. And herein lies the whole point of this chapter on activity within sales.

Unlike working in a factory, practising as a doctor, or even working in retail sales (where your work comes to you), the bulk of sales executives have to pick up the phone, knock on doors, and do the scary bit – cold call to bring a prospect [work] to them.

This is what I call *Activity* **Level One**. It is the more tricky level. Why? Because it is surrounded by various clouds of insecurity. Will I get another rejection? My last call was rude! I'll make another cup of tea and then I will get on to it. Blah, blah, blah. Before you know it, it is time for home, and you've just had another busy day doing nothing.

What's the cure for *'Level One?'* Acknowledgment. Acknowledge it, for whatever reason, and accept it as part of being human. Salespeople are people. It is okay to feel scared, hurt or disappointed. However, you need to manage it. Document your activity: keep a record of all your outbound calls, how many dials, how many contacts, and how many pitches or appointments you make. Only with this data, each day, can you start to properly track, reflect and improve on your activity. Imagine knowing this data on yourself! It takes me 50 dials of the telephone to speak with 10 (4 rude) people to make one sale, for example. With this data you become scientific towards your approach, knocking down any area of insecurity over cold calling activity because now you know, for sure, a sale (the warm, buzzy feeling and reason for doing this job) is coming around dial # 45+!

Level Two. This is all about your comfort zone. Let me explain this with one personal anecdote. Many years ago, I was a rooky sales executive selling advertising to retailers in London. The regional sales manager was shadowing me for my last call at 3pm. It went well and I made a sale. Better still, this meant I made quota.

A deep sense of satisfaction flowed through my body – I was in my comfort zone. *"Let's go back to the office"*, I said to my manager. But the reply was not to my 'comfortable liking'. *"Why? It's a 40 minute drive and it is only 4pm. Let's do an hour of cold calling whilst we are up here".*

Bam! And there you have it. He got me out of my comfort zone and doing what was logical: using my time to the maximum to sell and make even more money. I knew it was right, but it did grate somewhat. However, here's the oddity: by pushing me just a little bit harder, when my new 'comfort zone' arrived it was so, so much sweeter.

So, there you have it. Looking, feeling busy doesn't hack it. Doing the right thing, picking up the phone (or of course, actually working to engage that new Linkedin or 'social' contact), does. And unless you are keeping count of this activity – number of dials, contacts, pitches– you have no idea if you are just kidding yourself or actually making gains.

Only once you have this matrix can you overlay it with a skills improvement plan, at which point you start to climb the ladder into the super-league.

But let me end this chapter with an equally important point. I started with a reminder that salespeople are *people*. Well, happy people sell more. Fact. And monitoring your activity, as described above, will help you to identify when your working day has finished, and your personal time begins. This is extremely important because executives who work ridiculous hours burn out. I've known, watched, and employed the most 'busy' people doing nothing useful. Miserable as sin, working hard, doing the wrong things. Unless you address this demon, which is a perfectly natural demon within us all, sales will not be a happy place for you. But the good news is that now you've read this far, you know what to do!

Mark Blezard is a serial entrepreneur, starting his first publishing company aged 20. He has continued to spot opportunities and start various media and event companies over the last three decades.

He has always had a passion for sales, and consequently has led the sales efforts for all new enterprises and acquisitions he's been involved with. *"It is essential entrepreneurs learn how to sell their products before employing sales executives,"* Mark Blezard says, *"How else can you manage them? Moreover, it ensures you fully understand what you have created and how the customer engages with it."*

More recently, in 2015, he established Sales Skills Audit, now a leading online sales skills assessment tool used worldwide in all sectors. **www.SalesAssessment.com**

Notes

Chapter

5

Research Before you Call

By Jim Irving

"Research is creating new knowledge."

Neil Armstrong

When I do consulting work for larger corporates, one constant theme I hear from them as buyers is their annoyance at the number of salespeople they meet who are unprepared for calls and meetings.

We all know that being properly prepared is the right thing to do. You have now heard that the opposite actively annoys your prospects. So why not invest in preparation? In this chapter I want to look at both the bigger picture and at some practical tips I can provide for you.

Step 1. Let's start at the lowest level...

You are going to sell into a new marketplace. Perhaps you have had some basic training in preparation. If you haven't, demand that you get it. Could you imagine a plumber or surgeon turning up and saying *"well, I don't know much about this, but I will give it a go..."*. That's what we sometimes sound like – it hardly inspires confidence does it?

How exactly do you start with a new market?

Before you do anything else, learn about the market. Sounds simple and obvious, doesn't it? But so many don't. What steps can you take? Here are just some for you to consider...

First, learn how to use google alerts to receive news about the market in a form and amount that works for you. It's easy and very helpful. Once that's done, then try any/all of these -

- Ask your colleagues about the language that the market uses - terminology, phrases, descriptions - learn to mirror the language of your new market.

- Reach out to colleagues, friends, industry experts - anyone who has market knowledge. How did they succeed?

- Use Linkedin to ask for advice. What works and doesn't work? What's hot and not?

Why try to learn it all yourself when there is a world of information and help out there?

Use the above to provide a starter knowledge base for your entry into the market. And remember, success comes faster when you think clever, gain knowledge, and then work hard. Knowing your prospects' marketplace, environment and language is a great start. You then need to keep learning and up to date.

Step 2. Now you know the market, let's look at research for individual target prospects –

If you are targeting a specific organisation what can help you to create a strong introduction and a good prospect?

Think of the world from their perspective! Look for their statements on their business objectives - these can often be found on their website or, in the UK, from 'Companies House' - searches there are free. What is their CEO or Chairman saying about their strategy?

Scan their 'News' section - and google - to understand what is happening. Think of their world view being based on them being in a business 'mode' -

Are they just ambling along, 'business as usual'?

Are they struggling? Competition, layoffs, bad news in the press?

Are they growing - new locations, recruiting, new offerings?

Knowing this will help you to tailor your message so that what you say will 'strike a chord' with them. Ensure your messaging works for them. Mirror their world!

The first step to any successful engagement is understanding them, thinking like them, asking *"If I was them what would I be focussed on?"*

What other tools are available to you? First a comparison. At the start of my career, to learn about a leading bank I had to type a letter to post to their Company Secretary asking for recent information (it typically took around two weeks for anything to come back to me)! I looked up that bank recently and putting their name and 'news' into google delivered me 125 million results!

What else do we have available today? Here's a short starter list -

Google search

Google Alerts (as above, just look it up, it's a great tool)

Industry updates online

LinkedIn

LinkedIn Sales Navigator

Their website - focus on news and recent results statements

Their social media feeds

There is NO excuse for going into any call/meeting unprepared, but many are exactly that. So, stand out - be prepared and professional! Know their goals and challenges.

Step 3. Now, I have been asked quite a few times *"how much research should I do before I call or contact my prospect?"* That's a great question.

It's also a 'piece of string' one too! Before I go into my own tips, let me tell you a story. Over 25 years ago I was sent for some sales training. I was motivated and excited. I was selling mainframes for very large capital amounts in highly political accounts. More training would be great. It was an 'open class' training session with many companies attending. The training started OK, but the subject of how many calls into a target account was the right amount was raised. A discussion ensued. The trainer (whose only experience of sales was selling volume goods into pharmaceutical companies) said *"I can cut this conversation short. The answer is 4! Less than that is too few, more than that is a waste of time".* His limited experience had created a very rigid world view. The week before I had been in a target account five times and was worried that I wasn't close enough to my 20-30 contacts!! His inability to think about any other environment meant that his value to me was nil. I walked out of the training.

Why is that important here? Well, I could try to tell you how much research was right for you, but I would almost certainly be wrong.

If you are selling seven-figure products, solutions, or services then you had better be researching each prospect continually. You must be up to speed, following their news and actions, asking questions of everyone in there that you meet, and watching their market and world.

But, what if you are trying to sell much lower value offerings, in volume? No preparation is still 'just not acceptable'. So, what's the right amount? Or even the minimum?

To my mind it's simple. Do enough - every time, in every sector - to ensure you have at least a basic understanding of them and their market. Things like Director's names, their company products and business goals. Then at least you won't trip over at their first question...

Using the tools I mentioned above, I can find out the basics in around 10 minutes. That still allows you to deliver a good volume of calls each day. But I bet your hit rate will improve when you take that time out to research! Management shouldn't care so much about the call volumes, but more about the number of new prospects you are bringing to the table.

The lesson. Going into a prospect, or even calling them with no preparation is just plain crazy. No other profession would consider, never mind accept, that approach. The starting point is to know your market, then the prospect, BEFORE you reach out. You will be more confident, sound professional – and be professional. Once they have tested you (as they will) they will then treat you like a professional!

Notes

The B2B Sales Top Tips Guidebook

Chapter

6

Make it Easy on Yourself and Good Buying is Half the Sell

By Les Cairns

"Work smarter, not harder."

Carl Banks

I am delighted to have been asked to share a couple of tips from my half century of fun and satisfaction on the front line of business adventures!

"Make it easy on yourself"!

The 'Golden Rule' in sales is legendary – he/she who holds the gold, makes the rules! But getting to the ultimate 'rule' (or decision) maker can be an onerous challenge. Here's how I made it easier and a heck of a lot more satisfying and successful: Don't bother trying! What I mean is, at the outset, don't try to reach them directly, as you might not succeed. Even worse, in your persistence to win a bidding opportunity, you might aggravate the very key player you need. Instead, try this tactic for size, especially if you are selling B2B with a not insubstantial solution. When calling a new corporation, for a new bid opportunity, ask reception to put you through to the CEO's office and his / her PA (don't say "secretary"). In most cases you'll get through with ease. Tell her (Those PA's are still mostly female) about the project and ask her who would be the most likely executive dealing with it. If she knows, she will tell you. If she doesn't know, she will usually find out. If you're polite enough and ask, she might even put you through.

Taking an internal call from the CEO's PA is rarely declined (the psychology of this tactic is self-evident). If you're put through, you've already won a Stage 1 watch! The other plus is that the PA will usually opt for the most senior executive overseeing your pet project. If the project is being handled by a less senior executive, you will be referred or maybe even put through. Again, the psychology of this 'top-down' process is self-evident. If you're good, you're already well on your way to a positive introduction and you've met some key decision influencers on the way!

Some tips to remember when engaging with the PA: Be courteous and polite. Don't try to sell to her. Be genuinely respectful of her key role in the company. Be solicitous –

she is a professional 'know-all' and 'helpful' is her middle name. Her role is all about easing communication and enabling discussion. On more than one occasion I've even been asked to report back to her. But if not, do it anyway – always! A brief note of thanks is not only polite, it also wins friends! PS If you don't get put through but are given the 'rule' maker's contact details, always mention the PA's referral when you call – the same obvious psychology applies. You might even try cc'ing the PA but that risks a counter effect. Either way, always let the PA know how you got on – she too needs to feel part of a success story. To use a well-worn cliché, there is *"more than one way to skin a cat"* and this route to the key 'rule' maker has worked for me on countless occasions. Give it a try and *"Make it easy on yourself"*!

"Good buying is half the sell"!

As the new UK Sales Manager for a steel processing company, I was taken by the GM to meet the Head Buyer for a dry freight container manufacturer. Anyone who knows this sector, knows it is fiercely competitive on a global scale. On entering Tom Greenwood's office, the first thing I noticed was a plaque above his desk, which I've never forgotten, and which changed forever my perception of the buyer's role in enabling corporate success. It read *"Good buying is half the sell"*. At first, I confess I didn't get it. Then the penny dropped – this was no brutal signal that Tom was going to beat me down on price etc. It was a reminder to Tom (and by subtlety to me) that his success in procuring the best components at the most competitive price was critical to the successful negotiations of his own sales colleagues. I like to think I was quick enough to comment on the message – and without patronizing, told Tom that I respected his 'front-line' responsibility to win the best deal for his business. That simple acknowledgement helped cement a friendly and profitable relationship from then on. Tom ensured he got the best product from us, on time, and at a fair but competitive price. For our part, we kept – and increased our share of his business! Good buying is as critical to the bottom line as good selling. Professional buyers are not the enemy! They are allies! Acknowledging the critical role they play in their own corporate success, then playing to their tune in concert with our tune, is the basis of a sales/purchase partnership that is always win/win! Try to see buyers as being on the same side – not as opponents. Smart buyers know you too are in business to stay in business. That means offering them quality products and solutions at fair but competitive prices. Remember Tom Greenwood!

Les Cairns: Les has held several sales roles and also a couple of UK management spells in the engineering / manufacturing sectors before partnering with two start-ups, Sanmar Ltd and Ecosse Enterprises Ltd as sales/marketing consultant. Like seasoned actors, Les has "never really retired", but he spends a tad more time these days on his motorbike!

Notes

Chapter

7

Customers Have all the Answers

By John Convery

"Success comes from listening to your customers."

Richard Branson

They say timing is everything. Certainly, I was fortunate that I gained my MSc in Electrical and Electronic Engineering from Queen's University Belfast in the mid 1980s just as the microprocessor was starting to drive the shift to distributed personal computing, challenging the centralized paradigm that dominated the decades preceding.

A number of us worked in a unit of the University that provided advanced technical services to industry on commercial terms. This whetted the appetite and so it was straight from graduation and into business. The real world!

We started with no customers and little capital, but we were right on the leading edge of the hardware and software that was the basis of the IBM PC. There was plenty of competition from the likes of the multinational manufacturers – but we were convinced the journey to distributed computing was one we could lead.

Nevertheless, we were the upstart in this new Personal Computer market. Customer confidence (especially in the Public Sector) would be hard won. So, the sales approach from the outset was full service and cycle: find the potential customer (prospect), find out what they want (discover and then consult), give it to them (deliver), make sure it keeps working (support), bank the payment cheque (profitability) and ... repeat (grow). It was a technical and consultative sales process that was geared to gaining customer confidence from the outset.

So, from the get-go, the gene pool of the business was founded on the credo that 'customers have all the answers'. At that time, I was impressed with the Irish Supermarket entrepreneur Feargal Quinn and so his book 'Crowning the Customer' was a Christmas stocking read for all staff. I'm sure that got a big welcome around the family Christmas Trees that year!

Shift to Services

In time we recognized the need to shift from being primarily a PC reseller (hardware) to delivering much higher value services. This was to be a significant strategic move for us. It would require us to think and act totally in line with market needs to be sure that our investment in services was targeted, successful and sustainable.

The only way forward was to get customers to lead us to the answer. They have all the answers – we just have to be bold enough to go ask them! And then actually listen to the answers no matter how challenging. We initiated a program of customer engagement that was to lead to a number of advanced 'proof of concept' service contracts. From lessons learned in these, we would be certain of where and how we needed to invest to deliver what our customers actually wanted. The upshot was that out of this work – and very small start - we created an award-winning managed services business that helped us be one of the first of our peers to transform into a service-led business.

Many former colleagues have gone on to start successful businesses and careers and put their own version of 'customers have all the answers' into practice. I trained and worked over the years with many of the leading sales methodologies and techniques, all of which helped to add in one way or another to the pot in terms of improving our sales execution.

But the most potent concept of all remained the one we started with: ask the customer – they have all the answers.

So, what does all of this mean to you? How might my experience and outcome help you? Let's assume you are working for a corporate, or for the owner/sales leader in a smaller company. It doesn't matter which, the principle is still the same. As soon as you start in your role, go and speak to those who are already engaged with your prospects and customers. Most usually it is the sales, pre-sales/technical and customer support/success teams. In a small business it might just be a couple of people all told...

Ask them first, why do people buy from us? Then, what do they always rave about in what we deliver? Finally, what don't they like when dealing with us? Once you have this information from at least two sources, take some time to think about what you have been told.

Next, use that information, but don't take it as 'gospel'. Get out and visit your customers, ask them the same questions. Use good forensic questioning techniques to really dig down. What problems do they have? What worries them, keeps them awake at night? How can your offering help them? How DOES it help them today? What are the main things they like in dealing with your company? What do they like and dislike about their suppliers in general? Get all of this information and the detail of what they are saving or gaining by engaging with your company. Do this with as many customers as you can.

Often there is a disconnect. The value that your company thinks it delivers isn't what your customers see! It can be more, or less, or plain different. Only by speaking to your customers and giving them the time and space to tell you, do you know what your real value is – in the eyes of the only people that matter!

Now you are better prepared to prospect, explore and move new prospects along your pipeline; ready to bring crucial intelligence about the direction of customer travel back into your organization to inform future plans. Always think about what the user thinks is most important, best, or most valuable and then use that as you meet other new prospects. Use your conversations with existing users as 'ammunition' when you meet new prospects. *"It's funny that you mentioned this. Only a little while ago I was chatting to xx and they told me that was the biggest benefit they got from us...".*

Your customers have all the answers. They always have and they always will!

John Convery was Sales and Marketing Director at Belfast based BIC Systems, the largest indigenous IT services company at the time of acquisition by BT (NI) in 2004. Today John is a Belfast based angel investor in technology companies.

https://uk.linkedin.com/in/john-convery-849a7011

Notes

_____

_____

_____

_____

_____

_____

_____

_____

_____

_____

_____

_____

_____

_____

_____

_____

_____

_____

_____

_____

Chapter

8

Get your Priorities Sorted

By Jim Irving

"When you have too many top priorities, you effectively have no top priorities..."

Stephen R Covey

I covered priorities in both my first and second books. Why? Because it's at the core of almost all successful people. And we, in sales, are amongst the most driven to succeed, aren't we?

I am not going to replicate what was covered in those books, except to say that if you do happen to buy one of them, I used the same – fantastic – example of priorities in both...

Advert over, so what makes priorities, and the resulting goals, so important. Put simply, they drive our behaviour. Of course, if they are goals like almost everyone's New Year's resolutions then they are pretty worthless.

The priorities I am talking about here, help us to drive forward, to meet targets and to become more successful.

Let's look at a few approaches which can really help you to establish (and then later, review) your priorities and set realistic goals for yourself – and for your team if you are a leader.

Your first step is to take some time, get a sheet of paper and lay out what you believe your goals are. I would have no more than three, four at worst. Why? Because having twenty priorities means you don't really have any priorities!

Set out your goals, but not just as wishes – you can't measure them if they are vague. Always use SMART wording for your goals. (If you don't know the SMART acronym, just go on google, it takes goals and makes them specific and measurable).

Starting at the highest level, there are a couple of methods I have used to help me at the outset of the process – they both work, so just decide which feels the best fit for you.

The first approach to setting priorities and clarifying goals is called either 'The Eisenhower Matrix' or the 'Covey Quadrants'. Several people lay claim to this concept but whoever first thought of it is very clever. Thousands of variants of these are available online. I have chosen a couple at random, but I would encourage you to look for yourself. They all force you to consider your work and plans and then categorise them and act accordingly.

It is an incredibly simple, but effective idea. Let's start with a summary version –

THE EISENHOWER MATRIX

	URGENT	NOT URGENT
IMPORTANT	DO IT FIRST	SCHEDULE IT
NOT IMPORTANT	DELEGATE IT	DELETE IT

And now, here is a version with proposed priorities and actions –

	Urgent	Not Urgent
Important	**Quadrant 1** • Crisis • Pressing problems • Deadline driven projects	**Quadrant 2** • Relationship building • Finding new opportunities • Long-term planning • Preventive activities • Personal growth • Recreation
Not Important	**Quadrant 3** • Interruptions • Emails, calls, meetings • Popular activities • Proximate, pressing matters	**Quadrant 4** • Trivia, busy work • Time wasters • Some calls and emails • Pleasant activities

By way of an example, here is how I approached setting my priorities using this method, as a salesperson. I looked at what was taking up my time daily. I did this over a week or two. I then had my typical work pattern written down. Next, I looked at what my main goals were at the time – meeting target (of course!), improving my skills and career advancement. Then I looked at how much of my working time was spent on those things. Guess what, it only came to about 50%. Then I used the above process to categorise what I was doing so that non- essential things were delegated or ignored (or done outside working hours). Suddenly I had much more free time to focus on my priorities, my sales improved, and I started to make better progress on those other priorities too.

Go on, try it for yourself. It's very easy and incredibly powerful.

Another method to get to the same end point is Brian Tracey's 'ABCDE' priority setting method. Again, you start by writing down every single action or task you undertake.

'A' is the highest action category and 'E' the lowest. Again, going on-line will show you thousands of variants of this approach. But do look up Brian Tracy, I recommend his work. Here is one example of the approach –

A "A" stands for "very important;" something you must do. There can be serious negative consequences if you don't do it.

B "B" stands for "important;" something you should do. This is not as important as your 'A' tasks. There are only minor negative consequences if it is not completed.

C "C" stands for things that are "nice to do;" but which are not as important as 'A' or 'B,' tasks. There are no negative consequences for not completing it.

D "D" stands for "delegate." You can assign this task to someone else who can do the job instead of you.

E "E" stands for "eliminate, whenever possible." You should eliminate every single activity you possibly can, to free up your time.

Using either approach, you now have your work and priorities categorised. When it comes to time management you now must execute what you have put down. At this point I am always reminded of two core ideas, both of which make this all work.

First. 80/20 or 'The Pareto Principle' (after Vilfredo Pareto). I am sure you know this one. 80% of your revenues typically come from 20% of your customers. They also usually come from 20% of your sales team. Pareto seems to be a constant throughout business and nature – it 'just is'. Apply this to your objectives and priorities. Is 80% of your time and effort going into them? If not, then why not? How can you change?

Second. Eat the frog first. This has been credited to both Mark Twain and to Brian Tracy. It's a concept that is so sensible. Do you avoid that big, critical task? Too difficult? Too much? So much work? Well, here's the thing, if it is in the urgent/important quadrant OR a category 'A' action, then it's only going to get worse if you leave it. If you must do it and it's going to be hard, then do it FIRST. First thing in the morning, first thing in the week. Get the hardest thing done, everything else through your day or week is now better and easier. The supposed Mark Twain quote reads *"Eat a frog every morning, and nothing worse will happen to you the rest of the day."*

The lesson. Not setting your priorities and goals is a recipe for disaster. Set yourself clear, measurable goals. Execute a plan and focus on your core actions. This is the route to career and personal success.

Notes

_____

_____

_____

_____

_____

_____

_____

_____

_____

_____

_____

_____

_____

_____

_____

_____

_____

_____

_____

_____

_____

_____

_____

Chapter

9

Be More Collaborative

By Fred Copestake

*"If you want to go fast, go alone.
If you want to go far, go together."*

African Proverb

My sales tip for a modern sales professional in B2B sales is to be more collaborative. Use a collaborative selling approach. Why do I say this? If you look at the evolution of sales, we can see that for success today, we do need to be more collaborative than ever. It involves being consultative, and it is very closely tied to value-based selling. It involves having a personal brand, but we really need to be focusing on the customer, their buying process, and how we can work with them to create value. How can we do this? So, this is where I use a concept called PQ or partnering skills. That's not something I just made up. It's something that was researched back in the late '80s, early '90s, by a guy called Steve Dent. He looked at organizations that were good at partnering and then looked at why they did this and what the results were. For example, big airlines, who were bringing together informal business alliances and to cut a long story short, what his research showed was that it was the people who were involved, more than just the organizations. He then studied the skills that they were using.

He used the expression, which I now regurgitate a lot, which is organizations don't partner, people do, and he identified these six elements of PQ, which were then further validated and verified as the skills that these people use in the real world. So, if we look at them, they make so much sense from the perspective of sales professionals. And to be clear, I'm talking about sales professionals in direct sales here, as much as those in any form of indirect sales. What are these six characteristics?

TRUST. The six elements start off with trust. We've got to inspire trust in our customers. We really have to be trustworthy. It's not just us of course. We've got to be able to trust them too. So, we've got to know our stuff. We've got to do what we say we're going to do. We've got to be careful. We've got to be secure with all the knowledge and information that they share with us, but we've got to do all of this with that best intent in mind, we always need to be thinking about them and their needs and priorities. Our orientation has got to be towards the customer, not ourselves. That's the foundation that enables all of this to work.

WIN-WIN. We've got to have a win-win orientation. You know, we've got to be focused on mutual benefit. We've got to make sure that all parties are content and feel that they're getting a decent part of the agreement. We've also got to be comfortable with interdependence. What does that really mean?

INTERDEPENDENCE. Our success is going to be dictated by our customers success. Our success is also going to be based on our own team, our internal people's success. So, we've got to be comfortable that other people are going to play a part in what we do. Another of the six elements, relates to self-disclosure and feedback.

SELF DISCLOSURE AND FEEDBACK. So, this is about giving information freely about yourself. It's about sharing. It's about being transparent, being open, being authentic. This is letting people know what we need from the deal or what our expectations are. And this means we've also got to give honest feedback to customers. For example, if somebody's not working with us in a way that's helping us to help them. We've got to call them out. And yes, we also beat them up about it, but we've got to be able to say, *"look, we're trying to help you here. This is how the relationship should be working and it's not going according to plan. Which means we can't reap the benefits that we both want."*

COMFORTABLE WITH CHANGE. Another element of PQ is to be comfortable with change. It's simple, salespeople are change agents, and we've got to drive that. Status quo is ALWAYS our biggest competitor. We've got to be able to take that on and to help customers understand why they need to do something different. If we're going to do that, we also need to be comfortable with it too. Otherwise, we've got no right in talking to them!

FUTURE ORIENTATION. We've got to be looking forwards to really grasp what it is we're trying to achieve with our customer. What's the vision that we have together? How are we going to achieve that? And we make our joint decisions based upon that. Not looking backwards, not saying, *"Oh, this didn't work in the past."* This isn't something that is useful for us. We look forward, we make our make decisions based on our future plans and direction. We drive towards achieving those goals.

These six elements of PQ come together, work together, and they give us the mindset that gives us the ethos and the tools to operate in a far more collaborative way.

I hope you have found that useful. Hopefully, you can understand and then take on the concept of PQ. If you want to find more, please look me up on LinkedIn.

Fred Copestake is the Founder of Brindis – a sales training consultancy.

Over the last 22 years he has traveled round the world 14 times visiting 36 countries and worked with over 10,000 salespeople.

He has taken the things that really make a difference in modern selling and put these in his book 'Selling Through Partnering Skills'.

These ideas form the basis of his work with sales professionals involved in complex B2B sales to develop their approach and ensure it is up to date and has maximum impact.

He believes that people can get better through learning and sharing, and that with better collaboration we can really make a difference.

Notes

_____

_____

_____

_____

_____

_____

_____

_____

_____

_____

_____

_____

_____

_____

_____

_____

_____

_____

_____

_____

_____

Chapter

10

The Ego Trips
By Jonathan Crawford

*"Anytime you find yourself superior
or inferior it is always your ego."*

Eckhart Tolle

I stole this saying; it was not one of my own. It's a random meme I saw recently on Instagram or somewhere similar. But it immediately resonated with me. Especially from a career perspective. I was oblivious to this truth for 36 years! But as a sales guy, it took some major catastrophes, each created by my own ego, to make me crumble and then change direction.

I've had some great MDs and sales leaders that I've worked with over my 20-year sales career and the most honest and laid-back of them was the one who reminded me with a single phrase, *"Jonny, that's great work, just check the ego...."*

This was said at a time when my ego was about to be well and truly popped!

I always operated from the ego, I fed it and focussed on it, always *'what can I get?'.* I have seen lots of casualties – who were great sales guys and girls – do exactly the same. This issue seems to particularly impact salespeople.

Most, like me, always wanted more. More money, higher titles, always wanting things their own way. Authoritative, loud, wearing masks, never really expressing their true selves. Not building relationships in the truest form with their customers; always just thinking about the commission. When being successful, the egotistical salespeople just lap it all up, instead of being present and grateful for the team around them who helped them get there.

They are listening, but not really listening.

They have a one-track mind.

I'm not saying there's anything wrong with this approach for some, by no means. If you do want to be perceived to be successful and if you're strong willed and you want to put bread on the table and that's how you're conditioned, fine. It's a big bad world out there. But I've seen too many people, including myself, never prosper in sales (and in life) as a result.

Often this totally self-centred attitude ends up in performance discussions, disciplinary meetings or in the breakdown of relationships with those people you care most about and your colleagues. Some are focussed on just wanting to move to bigger and better, leaving everything you have built up to be left behind, even despite the conscious efforts you had already put into your own development in your current role.

Why does this happen? What's the cause? It's because the ego needs its fuel. That's why you see so many angry salespeople walk out of jobs, then try to do it better themselves and fail. They are always hunting and looking around for the next big career move. Their ego isn't getting the fuel it needs and craves. It needs its fix.

For me, to learn the lesson and finally to detach from and control my ego, to gain that awareness, I first had to crash and burn. Today I'll always have my values and I'll stand my ground. I've not gone soft. But I will always act in the humblest way I can. It was a harsh life lesson to finally 'get there'. There are many examples in my life, here's just one. And it's a perfect example of the lessons that drove my ego to pop, it was my final failure, in hindsight. When I started to "waken" from my life-long ignorance and from the error of my ways, I immediately decided to start a project that involved setting up a mental health charity and social enterprise. A lovely idea, I wanted to 'give back'. This project was aimed at helping others "awaken" from their slumber as well. The difficulty was, I just was not ready yet. Despite recognising my problems and wanting to help others, I was still being led by my ego. What happened to me? I was taking too much on. I was listening to the wrong people, I started to ignore my trusted advisors and mentors and I was lacking patience in executing my idea. My ego started to (again) drive me and I believed this work and outreach would make me famous! This was just so wrong for what I was trying to achieve. It was a mess. My plan (that I walked out of a good job for) fell flat on its face. I lost the interest I had worked to gain from people that had invested their time and money into the project. I guess I lost the whole concept of what I was trying to achieve, because my ego still made me believe I knew better, and I didn't have the humility to reflect on my mistakes or consider the direction I was taking. My ethos of what I now stood for in terms of always wanting to improve, went out the window and there was no way those other people could "steal" my vision. I had ultimately become deluded.

This situation resulted in me shedding 5 stones (70lbs for my American friends), completely turning myself inside out, going through some dark, dark places psychologically and spiritually, including being broke, out of employment by my own choice (rightly or wrong) and spending a couple of weeks in a local mental health recovery unit and then only after all that I finally recovered/surfaced.

I truly discovered that deep within, it was the continuous drive from my ego that was tripping and pushing me throughout my whole career and in my personal life. Let me tell you, it really screwed me up as well as impacting other people around me. And it wasn't until I got that inner awareness and understanding, that I can now see the same thing happening all around me with others. I guess I'm one of the lucky ones, who has experienced these lessons and behaviours to realise that the ego doesn't serve you well.

Eventually, I eased my way back into my career again although, at one stage, I felt that I actually needed to leave sales altogether as I didn't want to start to feed that ego again.

Then I had my light bulb moment...

This is when I observed that the very best salespeople in the world are the most grateful and humble. They have their goals which they pursue in a quiet and calm manner, making them known to only those who need to know. They slow down to speed up. They value and support their colleagues. They help and deliver value. They remember the small things. In my new life, my approach to a customer isn't *"what are you going to buy"* anymore. It is now *"how can I be of service?", "How can I help?"* I try to do this in the humblest way possible and I have become grateful for every bit of learning and insight along the way and for just being able to serve, learn and make my numbers more thoughtfully and professionally. And this attitude has helped me to be more successful, but in a much better and more sustainable way. Every human on the planet is a salesperson, they just don't know it! They persuade, sell an idea, negotiate, influence. I have realised this profession is where I belong as it's really about helping others. Now, I may or may not be successful in the long term, but with the right attitude and mind set I believe I will be. I will certainly be happier and nicer to be around! Because there's nothing feeding my ego and I'm not letting my ego pick away at my fear of failure (which it still attempts to do every single day).

I stand my ground and I know with humility and gratitude in my heart, I'll never crumble.

Don't get me get wrong, I'm humble enough now to realise I'm not always right. Of course, I am not, no one is! Some of the C-Suite players and CEOs seem from the outside to almost need their ego to drive them on. Perhaps some of them are aware enough to know how to use it in an effective and positive manner. I bet they are humble and grateful for that. And if they're not...then...my guess is that their humbler competitors might just overtake them – history tells us they often do.

My message is this, and it comes from painful experience. Be yourself. Focus on the long term and on long term relationships. Stay grounded and humble. In life and in business. Be content and happy. No one likes or seeks out the egomaniac...

Jonny Crawford. A father to two beautiful daughters, born and raised in Newtownabbey (a borough North of Belfast, Northern Ireland). I am a massive supporter of Manchester United. In my spare time I enjoy nature, working out, and invest my time in self-improvement by exercising, reading books, journaling, meditation, podcasts etc.

In my professional life, I am heading up the sales efforts at a great, local IT company, where I am passionate about helping SMEs to continually improve their processes and technology to help enable their growth and empower their people to succeed with best in breed business management systems. The best way to contact me is by email: **jonny@acornitsolutions.com**

If this story has resonated with you in any way, I'd be only too happy to discuss or help however I can.

Notes

Chapter

11

Discovery and Questioning

By Rick Denley

"Telling is not selling. Only asking questions is selling."

Brian Tracy

When asked how he was so smart, Albert Einstein would say

"It is not that I'm smarter than anyone else.
I'm just infinitely curious.

I stay with the questions much longer."

Staying with the right questions solves problems! High impact, intelligent, probing questions get the answers needed and discover problems and challenges others miss, which we then solve for our clients.

When coaching and training sales leaders and sales professionals, we are constantly striving to ensure the correct, up to date SKILLS + TOOLS + KNOWLEDGE are at the ready.

When discussing questioning, we are essentially using our KNOWLEDGE as a SKILL. So what objectives is DISCOVERY QUESTIONING looking to solve? And what value is it bringing our (potential) client? This should be first and foremost in our minds at all times, both as leaders, and sales professionals. We must consistently bring our sales team members, and more importantly our clients, value. When we do, they will continue to engage us in their business, simple!

So, lets look at the key objectives of discovery questioning. In fact, let's jump to the end, and ask ourselves the vital question; 'Do I understand the outcomes they're trying to achieve, and the obstacles in their way?'

Working backwards from this desired outcome, we seek to gain critical knowledge. So, we ask ourselves, how can I achieve this knowledqe?

The answer is deceptively simple, ask good questions! Want good answers...

When my son was very young and into superheroes of all kinds, he asked me: *"Dad, if you could have a superpower, what would it be?"* I thought about it for a while, aside from super strength, ability to fly and such, I answered *"To read people's minds."* Why? Because it would make things so much simpler in life, instead of assuming (which as the saying goes can make an ass-of U and me), we would just know what people are wanting, immediately! No miscommunication, no prying it out them. But we don't have this superpower. But there would be a catch with this even if it we did harness this superpower, that even with being able to read people's minds, it wouldn't help us fully because on many occasions our clients do not even know what they need!

So, again, how do we provide timely, innovative, strong ROI solutions for our clients if even they do not know what they need? Discovery questioning! We ask effective, probing, intelligent, industry specific questions to help us DISCOVER their true needs.

Let us take a brief look at the two different kinds of questions, specifically open and closed. Both have merit, if used at the correct time. Close ended questions, which generate a simpler, more direct answer, often of YES or NO, BIG or SMALL, or an accurate NUMBER, are very effective when prospecting and looking to secure an initial discussion with prospects. Open ended questions, which allow those you're communicating with to expand on their answer and take it in a direction they prefer, are excellent when in the qualification and solution seeking phases. A couple of examples of each:

Closed question: *"Is the morning or afternoon better to have a 20-minute discussion?"*

Open ended question: *"Share with me a little more about the challenge you spoke of that is hindering your business from meeting its potential growth."* Notice it's not even a question at all, just an opportunity for your prospect/client to share while you then listen and record key information, usually leading to the next question.

Developing New Skills for the New Era of Sales

Lifelong learning keeps anyone at the top of their profession. Let's take a closer look at how mastering discovery questioning can keep us there.

In another chapter of this book, Simon Hares shared; *"if you break down your questions into the key subject areas you must cover in your discovery call, then you reduce the chance of getting the objection from that area. For example, if you don't ask about competitors, then the objection will come from that area, if you don't talk about cost and budget then the objection will come from there, if you don't talk about the customers of the client, then they will find a way to use that as a base for the objection"*

So, what are the main areas you need to question to discover key information, so you understand how to solve your client pain points?

- Client perceived needs/problems/pain points
- Timing
- Budget
- Decision process, players
- Competition
- Past experience in this area
- Utopia – very best outcome

Questioning falls heavily under the qualifying stage of the sales cycle, initially, however it should be used throughout the selling process as newer information becomes available if circumstances change, as they often do. A colleague of mine teaches sales professionals to ask one final question at the end of each discovery meeting: *"Has anything changed since our last conversation?"* This helps ensure you're always up to date.

Learn, then Define: Instead of asking qualification questions, I suggest rethinking the traditional approach to actively listening. Replace questions like, *"Do you have budget?"* with more exploratory questions about your prospect's circumstances. Let them lead the conversation before you suggest solutions to their problems.

One area to be conscious of, however, is not to stop the flow of an answer from your client. Too often we are on to the next question without really hearing and thinking of the answer we've just received. After an answer, think to yourself;

Did I fully understand the answer? Does the answer make sense, or do I need clarification on what was shared with me? Do I need to stop following my preconstructed sequence of questions to dive deeper into my client's response? Follow-up, clarifying questions could include *"Does this then mean..."* or *"So how important is this to you and your organization?"* or *"Can you quantify that?"* In all your efforts of discovery, you also want to position yourself as an industry expert. Social media is a great way to create a following and bring value on a regular basis. In the 'discovery' stage of selling, asking the correct questions will bring value to your client and show knowledge beyond just your product and services. Asking questions that incorporate potential challenges your client is already experiencing, and some they may not have considered, or are forthcoming based on your industry knowledge, will gain you credibility and trust with your client. Often in my social posts on IG and LinkedIn, I start by asking a question related to potential challenges my prospective clients are facing, thus grabbing their attention. Check out some of my posts for examples.

Final word

Develop and stay with the correct questions as long as you need to. Have your questions prepared ahead of time, and some variance of them should the sales call go in a different direction than you anticipated. Sometimes, I've found it beneficial to even share your questions with your clients slightly ahead of time, thus they can give some deep thought to their answers, eliminating the "I'll think about that and get back to you" response.

Happy questioning!

Rick Denley, based in Toronto, is a business executive and entrepreneur who combines strong leadership skills along with coaching tactics with real world knowledge and experience to assess required organizational change that facilitates growth.

Rick's extensive background in transformational sales growth strategies, execution and team building has driven needed change in small to large organizations, including creating winning sales processes, focused on consultative and relationship-based selling. Rick's 30-year career has seen him lead Canadian divisions for multi-nationals based in Japan (Matsushita Group), France, (Schneider), USA (Emerson), and Germany (Phoenix Contact). Today, speaking on stages throughout the world, Rick's extensive background in transformational individual and organizational growth strategies, combined with his own life experiences, has driven positive change to thousands.

An advisor, coach and mentor, undefeated amateur boxer, and keynote speaker.

Peak Performance Leadership Services Inc.
T: 001 416 726-0173
www.rickdenley.com

Notes

_____

_____

_____

_____

_____

_____

_____

_____

_____

_____

_____

_____

_____

_____

_____

_____

_____

_____

_____

_____

_____

Chapter

12

Develop Yourself

By Jim Irving

"Personal development is the belief that you are worth the effort, time, and energy needed to develop yourself."

Denis Waitley

So much in life today is 'self-service'. The apps we all use every day on our phones help our banks, service providers and vendors to both reduce staff and increase their profits because they are outsourcing our admin to... us! It typically works well for both parties, which is exactly why the app-led world has become so popular.

We also often use self-service cash machines (saves tellers), self-service check in when we travel, self-service checkouts are increasingly used in supermarkets. In the UK and Ireland, at least, petrol (gas) stations have long since stopped filling your vehicle for you – you get out and do it yourself.

What does this tell us? It's simple, we are moving to an automated services/self-service world. This trend will only continue and accelerate.

If we bear all of this in mind, why then every year for the last decade have I heard salespeople say, *"the company just doesn't give me any sales training..."*. It's a common complaint. To be fair, it's justified. The amount, content and level of internal sales training has been dropping consistently for many years now. It's a serious problem. Companies are investing less in their salespeople. The result of this is, of course, pretty obvious. Professional sales skills and standards drop – and those harm businesses and their customers.

There is a lot in the world that we can't personally control. For example, the quality of our politicians (👎), educational standards, your customers, other drivers on the road. The list goes on and on. But here's the thing. You can't control them, but you CAN control how you respond to them. Let's say local politics is a mess. Do you mutter and complain, or do you get involved to improve things? Do you apply to sit on your children's school board?

We can do nothing and be unhappy or do something.
The same applies to our personal sales skills development.
A few years ago, it was pretty hard to do much. My choice
was buying cassettes from big name sales 'gurus'. Some I
bought were absolute rubbish; some gave me tips I still use
today. I could also read books – the same applied. Today,
things are different –

YouTube – a source of much training content. Of course,
it's not interactive but if you feel you need to 'upskill' in
negotiation and you go to YouTube and type in 'negotiation
skills' you will see a never-ending number of videos
available – again, the good, the bad AND the ugly! From
Harvard Business School to everyday people talking about
their experiences and everything in between. Take time,
watch some of the most highly rated - and learn...

TedX – another great source with some serious players
giving good advice. Watch some of the talks there - and
learn...

LinkedIn + the other socials – Very big variation in
standards. Start by following those authors and coaches on
the subject who have good reputations. The odds are their
posts will be worth receiving. They don't take much time
but help a lot. Read/watch - and learn...

Audiobooks – I prefer to read and take notes, but so many
people now prefer to learn this way. Sign up, use your travel
and spare time – and learn...

Blogs/podcasts – another world that's available to all.
I have taken part in quite a few. They are fun to do but
almost always focussed on just one or two topics, in depth.
The conversations bring out even more to help you. Watch/
listen – and learn...

The best in your organisation – in my example, find out who is the best at negotiation (could be in sales, or finance, or procurement for example), buy them sandwiches and take up their lunch break. Get tips, do's and don'ts, ideas – and learn...

I will have missed several learning opportunities that are out there. It's only the basic principle I am working to get over here. We are blessed today, there are so many learning routes. Each has its own strengths and weaknesses, and you must be aware that there is still rubbish out there – lots of it. But find the approach(es) that work best for you, be selective and... keep learning...

That only leaves one core question. What are my weaknesses? Where do I focus my learning first? I bet you have some ideas already. Ask your boss (in context!) and your colleagues. Speak to friendly customers. Once you have a settled idea of what you should be addressing first, then look for the content to help you.

At a summary level, the chart below sets out two core areas of skills for salespeople. This is styled on the likes of Gartner and others who operate this 'quadrant' concept. You want to be at the highest possible point at top/right. That's the goal. But be honest with yourself, *"where am I today"*? It's very normal for example, for new salespeople in a new job to get trained and become strong in communicating, but woeful in their knowledge – that makes for an easy decision on your own learning priorities! So, right now, think about where you honestly are on this chart. I have put in my suggested learning path from 4th to top. But your journey depends on where you are today.

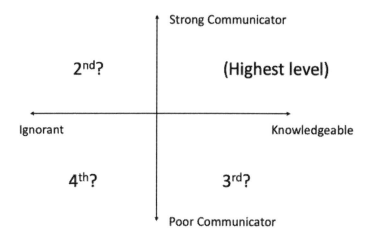

Whatever you do, do something. Don't wait for others, TAKE CONTROL and be proactive.

The lesson. In developing your skills and knowledge don't depend on others. If it's not happening or not enough, then go and find what you need yourself. Getting strong, ethical, professional sales skills and knowledge training from experts is the fastest and most comprehensive way to go, but all of the above routes will make you better and more able to succeed...

Notes

Chapter

13

Adding Value

By John Durant

"Try not to be a success, but rather to be of value."

Albert Einstein

Introduction

If you strip a transaction down to its basic premise; a business will want to pay as little as possible for a product or service. This ensures the business remains profitable by minimising its outgoings. We, as consumers, are wired the same way. Money is usually limited, and we want the best deal to stretch that resource.

By this train of thought – whoever supplies at the lowest price point should win every deal. If you are the cheapest, you will win more often than not, but the company you work for will suffer through its aggressive pricing and the subsequent reduction in margins.

Fortunately, there are factors that influence the cost of a transaction. For example, the level of service, the ability of a supplier to deliver, the future proofing of a product or service, etc. One of the biggest influences in a sale is the emotive element of a purchase. Due to social, environmental, or political reasons, a business may see additional value in purchasing from a specific supplier. There may be reliability considerations or technical innovations to give a business a competitive edge. All of a sudden, there are a whole host of additional aspects to a transaction that can increase the value and therefore increase the price point of what you are selling.

Then, there is the human element. People are emotive. They make purchases based on taste and fashion. They are influenced by marketing, advertising, and branding. They are not only driven by need and necessity, but by want and desire.

These are the grey areas in which a salesperson operates.

The best salespeople recognise value and articulate it in such a way to enhance their sales proposition and raise their own personal credibility with a customer. The very best salespeople become so valuable to their customers that they are no longer considered a supplier but a "Trusted Advisor."

So, as a salesperson, how do you add value to your customers?

Barriers to adding value.

The priority of a business is its primary function – a car manufacturer will want all its focus on making cars. Anything that distracts from that primary function could impact the number of cars produced.

As a salesperson, you will want to get to the decision makers, these are the people who sign off on a deal. The decision makers typically reside in the part of the business where the primary function is being carried out. Your customer could view your engagement as disruptive to that primary function and try to actively keep salespeople away from impacting their business.

Most organisations will have procurement teams, IT departments, Finance etc. They may have policies that state that over a certain spend, all purchases must go out to tender. To reach the decision makers, you need to make connections into the operational side of your customer, and this may be in conflict with the customers procurement team or IT department etc.

Your own company could be a barrier to adding value. You will be measured on what you sell. Companies selling commodity products can have a blinkered view on customer engagement. As far as they are concerned, your sales figures are your key metric and everything you do should be focused on achieving that metric. Any activities that are not linked to this goal could be frowned upon.

Adding value and becoming a Trusted Advisor may require a shift in mindset from your own company. The good news is, once you understand the principles of adding value, they can be applied to the company you work for as well as your customers.

Know Your Customer.

This sounds really obvious but knowing the strategy and priorities of your customer will allow you to tailor how you approach individuals within that business. There are the traditional fact finding and qualification processes you can follow to piece together this information – or you can cheat.

The best source of strategy information can be found in a Company Annual Report. You can usually find this on the company website under "About" and "Investor Relations". As documents go, they can be quite dry and lengthy. The juicy bits are the letter from the President/CEO and the Message from the Chairman. This will tell you everything you need to know about the company strategy and short to mid-term goals. All you have to do is align all your sales activities with these goals – Simple!

For example, if your customer is expanding into other territories, you could add value by demonstrating your companies offering in those territories, and such a strategic alliance would help minimise their risk by working with a known supplier with a track record of reliability.

Every sales course I have ever been on has pitched selling high. Here's the thing; unless you are selling something that helps the CEO achieve his strategy – the CEO will not have time for you. If you align your sales efforts to helping them achieve that strategy; they will give you their time – they can't afford not to.

There are businesses that do not publish an annual report on their website. If this is the case, ask a friendly contact for the company strategy document. Nine times out of ten, they will give it to you. This information will help you write your account plan. The insight and intelligence gained will add value to your own company by setting their expectations, and it will make you look good.

There is one department within every business that knows the company strategy, the company structure, culture, and can make introductions to practically anyone within that business. Not only that, but this department can also help you with your forecasting to help predict run rate. They are involved in change management and project implementation. They are involved in all of this, and yet salespeople rarely engage with them.

Who is this mystical department that can resolve all your engagement woes I hear you ask? That department is HR – Human Resources (sometimes affectionately referred to as Human Remains).

If there is a pie, HR has a finger in it. If there isn't a pie, HR will be beavering away to bake one. They are the gate keepers to everything and everyone you need if you want to add value to a business. HR rarely engage with salespeople, and ironically, this makes them easier to approach.

Note: I figured out the HR connection early within my career. This gave me an insight into labour levels, hiring, dismissals, and large projects. As a result, my forecasting had the accuracy of a laser guided missile. Upon moving to pastures new, my Sales Manager said in his leaving speech *"That most of all he would miss my forecasting"* – there is no higher accolade.

Problem Solving.

From the sales perspective, customer accounts are broadly grouped into three categories; Acquisition, Retention and Development.

The Acquisition salespeople tend to be the adrenaline junkies of the sales world that bounce from deal to deal, acquiring new customers, getting the contracts signed, and then disappearing off to a sales retreat to pat themselves on the back.

Although adding value should be the focus of every salesperson, adding value at a long-term strategic level is more often the domain of the Retention and Development salespeople. Especially with the goal of becoming a Trusted Advisor. (It should also be the focus in Acquisition, but so often isn't).

Things rarely go smoothly, from late deliveries (I once had two lorries of computer equipment destined for an investment bank impounded because illegal immigrants had stowed away onboard), to project delays, financial issues, you name it, and chances are it could happen. As a salesperson/account manager – you are the face of your company. Everything you do reflects on your company's reputation and your credibility as a professional.

That doesn't mean you personally have to resolve every issue that comes across your desk. You should pull in additional resource, delegate, and in some cases link senior board members within your company and your customer to hold senior level conversations.

In summary – get involved. You should be that single point of contact a customer can rely on to get things done. Never neglect the small things – they may be irritating, and seem like a waste of time, but a customer will remember what you do (or don't do!). The good news is, all problems have a silver lining once they are resolved. Customers will remember your efforts, you will gain their trust, and your personal stock within the customer's business will increase.

Problems are an opportunity disguised as a bad day. What is important is you are adding value by resolving issues. Whereas your Acquisition counterpart would grab the commission and run, you are in it for the long haul. Everyone remembers bad service; customers will pay extra for good service.

Articulate Value

Your customer will have a strategy, and individuals within the organisation will be working together to achieve a goal. A single sales value proposition will not resonate with all individuals within that business. Each individual with have different motivations (both personal and business related) that drive them to achieve their goals.

For example;

You have a widget to sell which is ten-times more reliable than the competition's widget, and it is the Customer Services Directors dream come true. The Customer Services Director is sold on the reliability.

Your widget is twice the cost of your competitor's widget. The Procurement Director wants the cheapest widget – he does not care about reliability.

The Finance Director wants the cheapest widget because it's cheap – he doesn't care about reliability unless he can see a direct and measurable payback.

You must demonstrate the value by showing the Finance Director that by spending twice as much on a widget, it will reduce his service costs by 50%, saving him 3x the cost of your expensive widget. This will improve the perceived reliability of his company's solution in the marketplace and thus increase their customer's own sales.

The Finance Director is sold. The Customer Services Director is sold. What is the remaining influence of the Procurement Director? (At this point you could replace the Procurement Director with a T-shirt that says, *"Can I have it cheaper?"*).

The point is this; everyone has a different motivation, so change your value proposition for your audience. Not just your value proposition, but also how you communicate. You may need to articulate a value proposition in a single sentence when talking to an executive over a coffee. You may need a punchy twenty-minute presentation to the board. An in-depth report may be required on the total cost of ownership and return on investment to the finance department. Add value by using the correct pitch to the target audience.

The Trusted Advisor

There is no job title or award that will let you know when you have achieved Trusted Advisor status. As an achievement it will probably be overlooked. So how do you know if you are a Trusted Advisor? Typically, you can look back on your career with the customer and realise how far you have come. When the company you work for realises that you are so key to the relationship that your removal would impact their bottom line.

Every so often a situation comes along where your expertise is recognised. You are the go-to salesperson that holds the relationship together. Your customer no longer sees you as a supplier – you have a contractors pass to their head office where you hot desk at your clients site. You spend more time with your customer than you do at your own company.

Then the nightmare scenario happens – you have gone through the sales cycles, done everything correctly, and the sale was awarded to a competitor. While your sales manager is flipping out; you pick up the phone, call a decision maker, and get them to reverse the decision. That's when you know you are at the top of your game.

Summary

This chapter has covered how to add value and where adding value can take you in terms of the relationship with your customer. Adding value should be systemic to everything you do. When you send out an email, make a call, attend a meeting, put together a proposal etc – ask yourself this question; would my customer pay for this? If the answer is yes – you are adding value.

John Durant has spent most of his working life in corporate sales within the IT and Telco industries. He has extensive experience within B2B and channel sales. He is currently running his own construction company, and also provides business and HR related consultancy services.
https://www.linkedin.com/in/johndurant

Notes

14

The Customer Journey

By Alison Edgar MBE

"Customers make it possible for us to continue with our business and its purpose."

Shep Hyken

In the world of sales, we are always so committed to 'us' and to 'our way'. What do I mean by that? We frame the world – and our prospects - in terms of what WE do, what WE need, what's OUR process. What are our sales steps? How does our CRM set things out? But we really should be starting with how customers in our marketplace buy. What their priorities and needs are and what their processes look like. Speaking logically, that makes a lot of sense, don't you think?

From my experience and research, here's what I think the most critical element – their buying process – most commonly looks like. I will explain each step and also talk about how the customer and the seller see that stage.

The sales process shows where you as the seller are in your own business terms, but what about the customer? Sometimes we find that the customer and the seller are on two different paths or at two different stages of the process, which is why when you try closing the customer might object. And frequently, their buying process doesn't even match your selling process – which of course leads to confusion and friction. It always makes the process easier if you ask the prospect in the early stages what their usual buying process looks like. Who is involved in that decision? What considerations do they need to make before buying? It means you're both on the same page, and you know what boxes you need to tick.

The customer journey shows us where the customer is in their decision-making process as it relates to our sales process. This applies equally in B2C sales and in the B2B environment.

When considering buying, the customer typically goes through eight stages:

1. I'm interested
2. Tell me more
3. You get me
4. I like what I'm hearing
5. We're a match
6. I want this
7. Wonder what it costs?
8. That works for me

Stage 1: I'm Interested

This is where you gain the interest of the customer. For many years I have enjoyed great success by using the '4 W's' approach. This involves four aspects to your introduction, with the real power lying in the fourth. Many salespeople tune and practice the first three, but then ignore the one that actually gains them the right attention and captures the prospect's interest –

1. Who are you? (Why are you calling them?)
2. Where are you from? (Who do you represent?)
3. What do you do?
4. **What's in it for them?**

Stage 2: Tell me more

This is when, as the seller, you are starting to ask open questions and conducting a bit of a fact find around the customer. You have retained their interest and now they want to know more about what you can offer them. Someone who is interested will have lots to say, so if they start to really engage with your questions, take it as a positive. Always remember to question carefully. Think about their first answer. Does that suggest an underlying problem, need or requirement? What is the logical next question if you don't just move along to the next superficial question?

Stage 3: You Get Me

Looking back at the sales process, this is when, as the seller, you should have understood their needs and used summarise-and-commit techniques to confirm you know what they need. When you do this the customer is thinking *"Yes, this person really understands me".* The customer appreciates the fact you have listened and understood their needs.

Stage 4: I Like What I'm Hearing

As the seller, you would have matched the benefits of the product or service to the needs of the customer. At this point the customer is gaining knowledge around what you are trying to sell them and, if done correctly, should like what they hear.

Stage 5: We're a Match

Now the customer understands what you can offer them and how your product or service matches their needs, they can make a decision on whether you're the right choice for them. Providing you follow the sales process they should see that you're a perfect match. Look out for buying signals at this stage!

Step 6: I Want This

Based on your recommendations and closing offer, the customer has developed a desire to buy. They like what you do, and they want it.

Step 7: Wonder What It Costs?

This is when the objections start to evolve in the customer's mind. They like everything you have said, and you almost have them, but committing to the purchase has them second-guessing themselves and justifying whether your product or service is what they really need and worth the cost. Here you need to be able to respond with value and benefit summaries to remind them of the measurable results they can achieve.

Step 8: That Works for Me

After some objection handling and negotiation, you have reached a win-win offer. The customer recognises the value of your product or service and goes ahead with the purchase.

It's important you understand how the customer journey works in relation to the sales process. When both run parallel, the process is seamless. The problem occurs when the two don't run parallel and the customer and salesperson are in two different places. When this happens, the salesperson usually sells too soon and the customer objects because they don't fully understand what they are being sold.

Two Become One

Now you are moving forward together. *"I genuinely believe when delivered correctly, sales and customer services are exactly the same thing."* This is a statement I live by and let me tell you exactly why. If what you're selling fulfils the customers' needs, then it's not sales it's customer service you are delivering. You are helping them to overcome their challenges and/or meet their goals and aspirations.

When I check into a hotel, my expectation is the receptionist will ask me my plans for my stay. By doing this they will uncover dinner in the restaurant and a massage in the spa would be right up my street. Yes, they are upselling their additional services, but at the same time providing me with a customer service. They have made my life easier. If you're a genuine fit for the customer and reach a win-win situation then it is a customer service.

That's why when I teach the customer service process, it's the same as when I teach the sales process. That's because when delivered correctly they really are the same. In the words of the Spice Girls, "Two become one".

Alison Edgar MBE also known as The Entrepreneur's Godmother is a twice best-selling author, entrepreneur, and speaker. She works with multi-national conglomerates such as SkyBet, Discovery Channel, and The European Commission, enhancing their development by encouraging them to think like entrepreneurs. Alison was awarded an MBE by the Queen in 2020 for her services to Business and Entrepreneurship.

Find Alison:

Twitter & Instagram	@thealisonedgar
LinkedIn	Alison Edgar MBE

T: +44 (0)20 3600 9967

Notes

Chapter

15

ETDBW

By Jim Irving

"The key to success is to be easy to work with."

DJ Quik

Some things in life are just so obvious that they hardly need to be said. *"Look before you cross the road"*. Some things are a little less easy to understand (like maths in my case, or exactly how electricity works). But there's a third group that are truly important, mostly ignored by the majority, but once mentioned everyone consistently says *"well, of course..."*.

This chapter is about one of the most important of that third category. And it directly relates to our business world – and to sales specifically.

I posted on Linkedin about this subject a few months back and this is an extended version of that post...

ETDBW???

Now, only a few, a very, very small number, will recognise this acronym. And I bet they all smile when they see it. For me it brings back happy memories.

Probably the best and most professional company I ever worked was for called Sequent. Now long gone into history (bought out by IBM). They had a set of values that they REALLY lived by. One of them was ETDBW.

What does it stand for?

Easy
To
Do
Business
With

This to me is one of the most important characteristics of companies (and people) who consistently succeed in seriously competitive markets.

Think for a second. How often have you been turned off by a poor engagement or buying experience? If it's happened to you in your own life, might it also happen in the B2B world? What does it feel like when you are hit by a simple transaction that's hard to complete?

Recently I wanted to send a small parcel to Spain. In fact, it was just a single key. I checked online and then went for the most local of the big multinational parcel couriers that operate across Europe (to narrow it down a bit, they have a three-letter name). The website experience was a bit 'm'eh', but OK. I am not dumb, but it took me a while to figure out that they didn't pick up small packages, I had to go to the nearest depot. Here the website was good. I put in my postcode, and it told me where the three nearest depots were. The closest was 12 miles away so I jumped into my car and headed off.

A while later I arrived at the location on a small business park. I searched and searched for their logo but couldn't see it. Then I noticed a building with what looked like the shape of their logo on it; just a shadow, the sign itself had been removed. The door of the building was locked and then I noticed signs all round of long-term construction work – inside and outside. 🏗️

Back in my car I called their customer service number. I explained what had happened. I was told there was nothing that could be done. When I 'suggested' that they change their website to reflect the fact this location was closed for the long-term I was told that *"it's not my role"*, but the person might pass a message along if they had time at some point that day. Ask yourself, with a big-name courier, how many people had turned up there over the months it had been closed? Where was the link between customer support and marketing? Why wasn't the website at least accurate with their most critical, basic information?

Back home and seriously angry I went online again. I found a company I can recommend to you if you are reading this in the UK – courierpoint.co.uk. They are one of those sites that does all the work for you. (Often seen in the insurance marketplace when you are trying to find the right policy). I told them what I wanted, they took care of all the admin, including emailing the recipient to give them an idea of the delivery time, they told me my small package would be picked up in an hour's time! The costs were much lower than the original company too. I was impressed and waited to see which company van would arrive for the uplift. I think you can guess – yes, the van that arrived to uplift was from the very company whose local depot was closed and who didn't do uplifts! They picked up the package at noon and it was delivered to a residential street in Spain at 11am the next day!

My original choice had delivered a world class uplift and international delivery. BUT their customer engagement was catastrophic. For my one small transaction they got less money, had to do the uplift and also pay a percentage to 'courierpoint' too. Imagine that multiplied by every visitor to their closed depot and lack of customer service. What a wasted opportunity. And finally, ask yourself, which one of those companies is now in my desktop diary?

Now look at your own personal sales approach and your companies' processes.

Would you like to buy from you???

What is that 'first touch' like for your prospects? How easy are you to engage with? If someone wants to buy from you, do they have to do all the work, or do you help and make it easy for them? Are your contracts clear and simple (in the UK at least there are several 'plain English' organisations that will radically improve your documentation for you)? Do you lay out clearly what the engagement will look like and help them at every step?

This is REALLY important stuff. Look back to the beginning of the chapter again. Remember this? "But there's a third group that are important, mostly ignored by the majority, but once mentioned everyone says *"well, of course..."*.

Yes, of course, ETDBW is critical, but are you? Really?

The lesson. Look at your organisation afresh. Ask your biggest customers what they like and don't like when they work with you. Ask for their ideas and experiences from dealing with others. The very worst that could happen is that you will see your weaknesses and have the chance to change, while they will be pleased you asked them...

Notes

Chapter 16

Resilience and Mindset

By Colly Graham

"A good half of the art of living is resilience."

Alain De Botton

Winston Churchill in a speech in October 1941 to the boys at Harrow School. *"This is the lesson: never give in, never give in, never, never, never, never—in nothing, great or small, large or petty—never give in, except to convictions of honour and good sense."*

Sir Winston Churchill was speaking about resilience – which is best defined as 'the capacity to recover quickly from difficulties.' My Dad taught me the importance of resilience in life and especially in sales. In 1948, when I was four, my Dad was diagnosed with MS, unfortunately he had partial paralysis which stopped at his waist. Then in the late sixties he had both his legs amputated due to infection, never once did I hear him complain or moan. He passed away at the young age of fifty-two and inspired me to become the person I am today. At the same age of fifty-two I started my sales training company, thinking of my Father as I approached that fifty-second birthday, I heard his words, *"Go for it, son!"*

Whilst my Dad demonstrated resilience in life, I did not make life easy for myself. In my late teens and early twenties, I suffered from mental illness for which I was hospitalised. My first marriage ended in 1969 after three short years and I found myself penniless on the streets of London. (I was running away from myself, but unfortunately, I had brought myself with me). There in London, I learned my first lesson in sales whilst begging on the streets. Someone heard me ask for sixpence for a cup of tea. They took me aside and suggested I should instead ask for the price of a hamburger, *"you'll get more money that way!"* How right they were and still are. When you are selling are you asking for a little money for a cup of tea, when you could be asking for the price of a hamburger?

I returned from London in the summer of '69 and decided to get a job in sales. After being told a few times to *"come back when you have experience,"* I landed a sales job with Pepsi Cola as a 'route salesman.' My mother was aghast that I was a lorry driver - which I was. I loved the job and was one of the few route salesmen who opened new accounts. This led to me being promoted to a brand salesperson, looking after key accounts in supermarkets. Unfortunately, at that time I was heavily abusing alcohol, which resulted in a few warnings from my manager. The franchise changed hands in late 1973 and I found a new employer in a start-up company selling to the hospitality industry. My drinking got out of control, crashing the company car more than twice, my saving grace was I was winning new accounts for this young business. I bought myself a book entitled 'Teach Yourself to Sell.' There was little in the way of sales books or any information on how to sell in those days (how different today). How my boss tolerated my drinking, I will never know. Until February 1974 when I decided enough was enough and I stopped drinking and decided to turn my life around. Up to today I have not felt the need for alcohol. I discovered a design for living, one day at a time. And that one day at a time was where my resilience kicked in, living in the day.

That one day at a time became useful when that same boss who saw something in me, made me sales and marketing manager of the sales team. How was one day at a time useful? I had each member of my sales team set themselves daily goals and it worked a treat and in a few short years we were winning a major share of the market. With the CEO of the company, we formulated training for our sales team incorporated with kerb-side training. Of course, I realise today this was sales coaching.

As the sales team needed training and in a hunt for sales training material in the early eighties, I discovered Tom Hopkins and his book, "How To Master the Art of Selling." I went as far as buying Tom's cassette tapes (yes, cassettes!) from Nightingale Conant for my sales team. Later in the eighties I discovered Brian Tracy and "The Psychology of Selling." So, I then used Brian Tracy's video tapes to train my team.

The more I was involved with training my team, the more our success grew, I really enjoyed coaching and training the sales team. You know what, like a lot of people I then moved to an island called *"Someday Isle,"* many people live there! *"Someday I'll do this".* I dreamed about running my own sales training company. It finally came about in 1995 when after a visit to the USA, on the flight home, I wrote a goal, *"I will start my own international sales training company"* and one year later in July 1996 I took the leap of faith. It's been a great success!

Yes, I still read sales books, I still want to learn, even after all this time. I am frequently asked how sales have changed in the fifty years I have been involved in selling. The only notable example is how better-informed customers are today because of the internet. Are there any new sales ideas? Not really, just old ideas, perhaps presented in a new way. As salespeople we have always had to provide insight to educate, collaborate and then convince our customers and of course sometimes we must challenge them. We have always had to build relationships, offer solutions, and add value, and that is what we need to do in selling - one day at a time.

Resilience is core to success. I know for certain; I am that man...

Colly Graham brings many years of practical experience of selling, his ability to empathise with salespeople, thus establishing immediate rapport and credibility as a trainer. His training is state of the art as Colly keeps abreast of the latest trends in marketing and selling. In 2014 Colly Graham was recognized by The Institute of Sales Management, at The British Excellence in Sales & Marketing Awards (BESMA) and has been listed in the top eight sales trainers in the UK.
www.salesxcellence.com
www.on-sales-online.com

Notes

_____

_____

_____

_____

_____

_____

_____

_____

_____

_____

_____

_____

_____

_____

_____

_____

_____

_____

_____

_____

_____

_____

_____

_____

Chapter

17

Strategic Sales – The Golden Key, a Proven, 7-Point Battle Plan

By Jim Green

"Strategic thinking rarely occurs spontaneously."

Michael Porter

(How small teams can win large deals against the biggest competitors.)

"An army's effectiveness depends on its size, training, experience and morale, and morale is worth more than all the other factors combined".

Napoleon Bonaparte

A major opportunity surfaces. You are in a small company faced with several large competitors. They have seemingly overwhelming advantages – large offices in multiple countries, major reference accounts and an army of staff resources for product development, marketing, and sales muscle.

Selling is like submarine warfare. You cannot see your opponent, you cannot hear your opponent, and you don't have much idea about what they are going to do.

Deep down, you know that you must go for it because if you don't, you will never forgive yourself. More importantly, your team and company may never forgive you. You know that winning can transform you and your company's fortunes, but ask yourself, how can you possibly make that happen? Sound familiar?

It should do because that is a question most salespeople have asked themselves at some point in their careers. Salespeople in large organisations wonder, *"how on earth did that small competitor beat me to win that huge deal?"* Many will take that thought to their retirement graves with no answer.

Let me tell you what happened - they just came face to face with their worst enemy - the company they underestimated. Even with all the advantages big companies have, all you have to do is be better, but how can you do that against those big teams?

Your first 'advantage' is that nobody will be taking your (small) company seriously. Your competitor may never even have heard of you. Even if they have, it's likely they won't be paying that much attention because their telescopes will be focused on their main threat - the competitors they have been up against in their battles for market supremacy over previous years.

So, what can you do? Your goal is, of course, to win your first big battle - the one that nobody really thought could be pulled off. The next step is to use that first win to build your team's belief in you because **morale is the child of belief.** The definition of belief is: *a state or habit of mind in which trust or confidence is placed in some person or thing.* The result, as Bonaparte knew, is Espirit De Corps.

Remember this – once is an accident, two is a coincidence, and three is a trend. When you have proven a trend in sales, you will never be alone again as a leader because your team will also aspire to be like you.

Your prospects team won't all share the same vision, so make sure you laser focus on the right individuals – the one or two senior management decision-makers and influencers who believe you best understand their vision and can deliver it.

So, here are those 7 steps to success –

Step 1 – Identify a 'frighteningly' large target
If the size of your prospect doesn't frighten you, then they're not big enough.

Make sure your prospect has a legacy problem and doesn't have an existing vendor capable of delivering the perfect product or service solution to them. If your prospect does and they are happy enough with them, you'll probably face an uphill battle that will waste a lot of your valuable time. Your call.

Step 2 – Find a Point of Entry

A point of entry is your starting point, and the best place to start is to identify a mid-to-senior person who is internally respected and has a direct connection to the Board. The ideal characteristics are a strong personality, self-opinionated, 'bulls**t averse' and courageous. The kind of person who has the best interests of their company at heart and no 'career fear' in saying what they think. Senior people really listen to honest staff who have earned their trust.

Step 3 – Present your <u>first</u> Compelling Business Offer

The objective here is simply to get **to the starting blocks in the race** to buy time to make your second (final) offer. Be open to your prospect that your company is smaller and can't match your competitors' resources in offices or staff - they will know that anyway. However, what you can offer is valuable to the prospect, delivering a role to them as the 'unknown outsider'.

Explain that having an unknown underdog vendor in the race has three benefits to the prospect. **The first** is that it will shock any complacency out of the large vendor(s) because they have no idea why you were even allowed into the race. **The second** is that it will help drive down prices because big vendors will have a reasonable idea of their competitors' pricing but no idea of yours. **The third** is that it will stretch the efforts of all contenders and improve the prospect's selection pool at no additional cost or effort to the prospect.

Make it clear to your prospect that you are realistic about your much lower chance of being awarded the contract but are happy to take that risk because of the value to your team in getting the learning experience.

Step 4 – Assemble and brief your team

I've often been asked, *"but how can a small company possibly beat the big players".* The answer is simple: to grow a small company, you need to make sure your sales team is great because one expensive failure at the early stages of a company can mean death.

Companies with multiple offices and sales teams can take a few losses, **so the average competence of competitors' teams will reduce as the number of sales teams they have grows.** Except for a few examples, big companies can't have 'A' teams everywhere because there aren't enough 'A' sales professionals around to do that. Your 'A' team can therefore beat the majority of your competitor's 'B' and 'C' teams. **Trained properly, your team can be as good as your competitors best and better than their average.**

Make sure your team sticks to their roles, there are several –

The first is called the **'Mad Scientist',** the individual who 'loses' everyone in the room with their technical competence. They don't have to be mad, and they don't have to be a scientist, but they do have to be extremely good at explaining how beautifully your product works and delivers results for customers.

The **'Technical Guru'** is the practical person who works closely with the customer and has the knowledge and experience to turn the customer's dreams into reality.

The **'Helpful Sales Exec'** orchestrates the whole process and provides the 'business chemistry' in communicating and building trust with the customer – the business executive who understands and cares about the prospect's business pain.

The **'Rounded Pre-Sales Expert'** is seen by the customer as the honest broker who confirms to the customer what the salesperson has said and handles the details.

Everyone on the team should provide 'covering fire' in presentations and meetings. This means each person in the team linking their information to customers back to reinforce information from other members of your team, providing mutual support - all linked to the key business points. Always carry out 'premortems' (as I call them) and postmortems for every customer meeting.

The overriding objective is to make your prospect say, *"You folks really look like a team"*.

Step 5 – Buy Time, Earn Respect and Build Confidence

Be first to respond to the prospect at every stage. Prove everything you have said and, if possible, provide a personal stake/outcome for every person on the prospect selection team. A personal stake is something that will never make it to the prospects business requirements specification but is a personal wish of each individual on the selection team. Finally, keep prospect contacts alive through regular calls.

Step 6 – Stick Close to The Deal

After you have reached the shortlist, fear of project failure (and subsequent professional embarrassment) is the greatest motivator of your prospect. **In this step, you are selling insurance, not functionality.**

The prospect's insurance is that **you have clearly shown you are the most committed vendor** because you have built that trust with the prospect. However, don't underestimate your competitor at this stage. They may sense that the deal is slipping from their grasp and take desperate measures such as flying in senior executives (as IBM often did) or offering crazy price cuts. Be aware that **the danger of losing your deal increases as the time available to close the deal decreases.**

Step 7 – Make the final Compelling Business Offer

The Magic Sales Number here is 3-3-1

The <u>three</u> things you are offering for the ***Board*** are **shareholder value, lowest cost of ownership and speed to market.** However, **the selection teams won't necessarily value what board members do** and here are the reasons why. Selection team members will often not have any shares in the company, the lowest cost of ownership does not affect them personally, and speed to market means tighter deadlines, more pressure, and less time to do the job the way they want.

The <u>three</u> things to concentrate on for the ***selection team*** (who will be making the recommendation to the company Board) are **your world-class product, the certainty of your commitment and confidence in you being flexible when unforeseen events arise** (Boards of directors expect all the things you are offering the selection team anyway).

The reasons for the above are that implementing a world-class product is great for their CV, and they need your commitment because they don't want to be left 'carrying the can' alone when problems occur. They need you to be flexible when the unexpected happens, and they don't always have more budget to cover it.

The final, <u>one</u> unexpected thing the **selection team** gets free is that you are seen as the most fun company to work with. If they enjoy your company and approach, they will subconsciously prefer you.

Game Shift has now happened near the end of the process

The competitors were front runners, and you were unknown. You have set the agenda on shareholder value, speed, and price. The competitors set their agenda on their projection of the notional 'security' of their big company. You have verified your capability, and the competitors remaining on the shortlist now have to justify the higher price they will undoubtedly be charging.

You have maximised the element of surprise. Did the competitors underestimate you? Were they arrogant? Let's hope so!

Avoiding the 'Project Rapids'

There are a few things you have to monitor all through the sales and project delivery processes. These include poor understanding of business requirements, aiming too high in any single sales cycle, unnecessary complexity and the availability of data and schema from legacy systems that you can never fully evaluate until you get the information.

The Golden Key

You have the Golden Key when at any point in the sales cycle, you know that you are in the lead. Despite what anyone may tell you, you must assume that **a decision-maker is always ready to choose a vendor.** You have the Golden Key when, at any instant, you are their personal chosen vendor.

You know when you have it. You may also feel you don't have it. If you are unsure, assume you don't have it and take immediate remedial action to get it back.

I wish I could give you more details on the process and real examples of how this works, but there simply isn't space in this chapter. However, I hope it makes you think and be inspired by what is honestly possible.

Buy time to gain trust, have a good product and charge a fair price, but it will ultimately be trust that finally leads you to success.

After all that, remember that if you have any integrity, want to sleep at night and tell your kids the answer to what you have done in your work life, this is not just about you; it's also about the people (in your own team and in the customer) who put their trust in you. That should be a fundamental part of your commitment.

You will have earned the trust of your customers if you do what you say, and **never forget that your success is based firmly on theirs.** If you remember that, you will firstly be a better person and secondly a better salesperson, which is the right order.

Finally, remember:

"If there are only two possible options, your opponent may choose the third"
Napoleon Bonaparte

Jim Green is Chief Executive Officer and co-founder of Spartan Solutions Ltd, an award-winning UK software company specialising in mobile digital operations and artificial intelligence solutions for the global rental, energy and renewables markets. Jim has over 40 years of senior management experience in major software companies and has worked extensively in the UK, France, Sweden and the USA. See **www.spartansolutions.com** for more details.

Notes

Chapter

18

Objection Handling

By Simon Hares

"An objection is not a rejection, it is simply a request for more information."

Bo Bennett

Getting to Yes by Welcoming the No's

'No' Doesn't Mean Never – it just means 'not now' – yes that's right people, we have reached the part of the book that helps you get over those dreaded objections. In my thirty years of sales, I have read about, heard, and tried so many different techniques for handling objections in sales. Some are good; some downright butt puckering and others are just plain rude. There is one approach however that really stands out to me. It's not a smart phrase, although there are some good ones out there (I will share a couple); it's actually a mindset thing. As salespeople, objections shouldn't be dreaded, they should be welcomed. Let's think about that for a moment. If a client can put together a series of objections to give to you, then that may well take some effort on their part, so why would they put any effort into talking to a salesperson if they weren't interested? If you were to think about a normal conversation outside of sales, we regularly put up arguments or reasons not to do things. It's how we hold conversations, and we don't dread that, so why would a sales conversation be any different?

Let's just be clear for a moment, clients will object because they can, simple. The key is listening out for objections coming in the conversation, anticipate them, predict them, and be prepared for them. Then when they happen, deal with them. No doubt you may have also heard that a client will say 'no' to a salesperson any number of times before they say 'yes'. I have heard it's twelve times, although for me I think it's closer to seven. With that in mind, you better get used to having to have these conversations, right?

The 5 categories of objections.

If I asked you to list all of the objections you hear from your clients, I suspect your list would contain a lot of examples. The reality is that often we can group these objections into a category; after all there are an infinite number of ways for a client to say *"we have no budget"* right?

It's a bit like nursery rhymes; think about this, what do Baa Baa Black Sheep, The ABC Song and Twinkle Twinkle Little Star have in common? That's right they all have the same tune. Again, how many ways are there to say no budget? Different words, same tune.

It is well known that people buy from people; well, in fact, people buy from people who they trust, like and believe to be more specific. They also like salespeople who think like buyers and do so with a view to helping them to make money, save money or reduce their risk. With this in mind, we can establish that if none of the above is fulfilled then that may be where your objection will originate. Here are my 5 categories of objections -

Source 1: You
If clients buy from people they trust like and believe in, then you need to work a little harder on winning people over with charm, sincerity, and warmth. You will also need to demonstrate that you know your stuff so the client recognises you as someone credible, and when you can back up your claims then you don't come across as a risk. We hear a lot in sales training about building rapport, well its so much more than just small talk.

Objection examples:
"I am not sure your company understands what we are looking for"
"At this point we're going to stay as we are, but thank you for coming in"
"I guess we'll give it some thought and come back to you"

Source 2: Price
Sales professionals, who truly understand the meaning of the word value, rarely get this objection. You see clients want to work with people who want to genuinely work with them too and are worth investing in. If your solution doesn't represent or demonstrate value, then price will be the objection. Value is defined, as the worth a person attributes

to something, be it financial, material, emotional, spiritual or aesthetic. Think about what you are selling in terms of clear benefits and ROI and work hard to demonstrate it.

Objection examples:
"We don't have any budget right now"
"That price is a lot further away from what we are used to paying"
"I know I can get what you offer cheaper, and I can get it faster"

Source 3: Differentiation
Let's face it; there is a chance that what you sell is available from other people, in various degrees of quality and at different prices. You are part of a marketplace that buyers can shop from. When we differentiate ourselves effectively, we don't slag off the competition, we acknowledge them. We don't become defensive about clients considering or using the competition, we welcome it. At least they are buying from the marketplace; salespeople can often forget that small point. I have a technique I use with clients when they ask me what makes me different. First, I say *"on the surface probably nothing, sales training is sales training, however what makes me relevant to you is that I am a sales professional first and foremost, and that just like your salespeople, I am going through what they go through every day. That will make what I train relatable and relevant."* That word 'relevant' is the differentiator, try using that a little more and see what happens. Everyone says they're different, but not many talk about relevance.

Objection examples:
"We are going to be looking at other companies too as we want to shop around"
"Your competitors have come up with similar solutions, we will have a think and come back to you"
"It doesn't feel like what you offer is any different to what I am already using"

Source 4: Timing

The planets don't always line up in your favour, the days of getting a sale first time can be rare. Sales can be a rollercoaster. One week everything you touch turns to gold, the next everything you touch turns to...well you know what that word is! At the start of this chapter, I wrote 'No doesn't mean never, it just means not now". When a client says 'no', maybe at that point they are really saying *"have another go"*, *"try a bit harder"*, *"let's see what you're made of, come back with something else, something different, something better"*.

Objection examples:
"It is the wrong time of year for us to be moving suppliers"
"My budget is spent for this year, perhaps call me back in six months when the timing is better"
"We wouldn't be wanting to do anything until at least the New Year"

Source 5: Risk

If you don't have the proof, evidence, and information to back up your claims then you can fall flat on your face and create a risk to the client. Always have information that can act as proof, to substantiate all your claims. Use testimonials from other clients, use analysis and research to support your claims, demonstrate proven results using accurate and up to date data. Salespeople who don't back up claims just end up with clients giving the objection *"we are happy where we are thanks, we won't risk changing right now."*

Objection examples:
"I am not sure that the information really supports what you are saying"
"I think we will probably look to stay as we are right now and with our current supplier"
"This may involve too much effort and I am not sure I want that right now"

3D Objections and Tools to Help

I mentioned earlier that we could predict what clients will say in terms of objecting. A behaviour I have noticed I call the 3D effect. It stands for Deny, Defend and Deflect. Clients tend to do this subconsciously when talking to salespeople. It goes like this.

Deny – *"I am not sure we are ready to move forward with you just yet...."*

Defend – *"...and that's because we want to talk to our current supplier first about what they have..."*

Deflect – *"...so with that in mind is there anything else we need to discuss?*

Or

"...I am sure you hear similar things from other clients too, right? What sort of challenges are they facing?"

Did you notice that the deflect stage can be done quite directly or it can be done quite softly in both examples? This behaviour is so common and can be avoided with a couple of simple techniques

1. Questioning

Rick Denley talked earlier about the importance of discovery and questioning skills. If you break down your questions into the key subject areas you have to cover in your discovery call, then you reduce the chance of getting the objection from that area. E.g. if you don't ask about competitors, then the objection will come from that area, if you don't talk about cost and budget then the objection will come from there, if you don't talk about the customers of the client, then they will find a way to use that as a base for the objection. So, cover off your subjects and minimise the objections coming out in the first place. Think about the objections you currently get and work out the subject area they have originated from and how you can prepare better questions with future clients to reduce the chance of it coming up.

2. Present the Objection before the Client Does.
I often hear people say that buying training is expensive and if I don't cover it off quickly then it can be a sticking point. Instead I often preempt the client by saying *"You might be thinking that sales training is expensive, and you would be right, it does require significant investment in time and money, however, the right sales training delivered by a relevant trainer can make such a difference to your teams skill levels, their morale and of course their conversion rates, so let's talk a bit about what you are looking for in more detail."*

By doing this it takes the wind out of their sails and reduces the impact of the objection because you thought it through and were confident enough to face it. Look at the 3D example above and think about how you could present the objection first like I did with price.

3. The Classic Feel Felt Found.
This is one of my favourite techniques as it just works so well. When presented with an objection, let's say "I want to discuss this with my current supplier first before we commit" we use 'feel, felt, found' to really show our levels of empathy and understanding of the client situation. I cannot over emphasise how effective this classic technique is.
*"I understand I how you **feel**, I would want to talk to my current provider too,"* this tells the client, that you agree, and that understand where they are coming from. It is an empathy thing.
*"Other clients who have moved to us, have **felt** the need to do a similar thing".* This shows that you have heard it before, that it is not uncommon and that you are prepared to wait for them to do that. However, you do need to move things to the next stage, which is where the final step comes in.
*"What they have **found** is that once they have had that conversation, it is a very quick and easy process to transfer to us as your new supplier and start enjoying the benefits of what we can deliver to you. We would be*

delighted to help walk you through that process once you have had the call"

Have a look at some of the other objections I have listed and see how you could use this technique. It is also worth noting two extra benefits that you gain when using 'feel, felt, found'.

1. The client doesn't 'feel' it being done to them. It is very conversational and natural, just as you would use the same language when offering help to a friend. *"I understand how you feel, I would have felt the same way, but what I found was that just by talking it through like we are now, that it can make things easier to understand."*
2. It works in the written form too, so if you must address objections with solutions and solving problems it is pretty near perfect.
3. Using video messaging is a great way to apply this technique, as you can really put across the solution in your message, and it feels (that word again) very personal and specific to that individual.

These are my favourite approaches to objection handling, and I hope you find them useful.

Simon Hares has over 30 years' experience in sales and management, and is now the founder and Managing Director at SerialTrainer7 Ltd. For the last seven years the business has delivered sales and management training and coaching to businesses all over the world in sectors including media, medical, hospitality, finance, workwear and videogames.

Proud to be a part of the sales community, Simon is an active supporter of sales authors from around the world and can be found on LinkedIn posting tips and techniques to help sales professionals become even better. Simon has been married to his husband Matt for the last 28 years and out of hours he can be found with his nose in a book, a Playstation controller in his hand and his dog Lundy asleep on his lap.

Notes

19

Selling in a Covid/Post Covid World

By Jim Irving

"Hard times don't create heroes. It is during the hard times when the 'hero' within us is revealed."

Bob Riley

As I was completing my second book, Covid was raging around the world, for the first time. It prompted me to write an appendix with my thoughts on the impact it may have in the future.

Today we are seeing changes in society, business and sales which are direct results of Covid and the impact of Covid on markets and vertical sectors.

COVID has had an enormous impact, but what about selling, post-COVID or, more accurately, living with it? I have been observing changes throughout the pandemic and I have also been speaking with my clients – across many sectors and geographies – about their experiences. Here are my thoughts -

Along with my clients, I have observed several consistent trends...

1. COVID has destroyed much of the 'you have to be there to sell' story. If your company sells in volume and at lower cost, then Zoom et al are now the proven way to go. I don't see that changing much at all in the foreseeable future. This means the lower level 'territory', high volume/ low value sales roles are constantly under review. Reliable revenues are now more critical than ever before. If revenues drop then there will be a fast and serious review of a territory versus phone-based role.

2. If you sell big-ticket, complex solutions then I now see a two-tier approach. Smaller deals will move (and are already moving) to zoom most or all the way. Larger deals, where you still need to work those corridors, manage the politics, and gauge sentiment and attitude continue to need on-site presence and work. However, at the early stages, almost everything (both large and small) is increasingly online, until the first qualification phase is completed, and it's confirmed that the deal is both real and large enough. That will apply to all sizes of B2B deals across all market sectors.

3. The need for qualification to justify travelling, combined with your Finance department now seeing that at least some sales can be made online, is going to bring more pressure to sales professionals. Qualification and spend will be much more tightly controlled and so, to be blunt, will become a much bigger hassle for salespeople and the related workload will increase.

4. The first three points relate to my direct findings. What are the analysts saying about the situation now? I have, on your behalf, done the research legwork and can now report, to add to my own findings, from several sources –

5. Tom Tunguz (active on Linkedin and worth following) recently engaged in a conversation with Jim Benton, the CEO of Redpoint Office Hours. The findings were interesting. As a result of primary research here are some of their findings...
a) salespeople are inviting their managers more frequently to meetings (perhaps because they are now even more critical?) and this has had the impact of improving the average conversion rates by 34%.
b) More zoom-type calls are required to close enterprise deals than meetings. (I think this makes a lot of sense).
c) There has been a significant rise in the successful use of storytelling (references, examples etc) in closing business. (Perhaps after the isolation we are all craving normal conversation?).
d) Finally, there has been a rise in so-called composite meetings, with some physically in the room and others joining online. (This gels with my experience – it's become a new 'thing'). Overall sales efficiency has dropped a bit (understandable) and the data does point to lengthening sales cycles, lower conversion rates and some of the traditional travel budget moving to online and social marketing spend.

6. Gartner recently completed a large-scale study. They found that more people from the buying organisation are getting involved in larger decisions. Their averages showed that for 'larger corporate purchases' the number of people directly involved has grown from 5.4 to 6.8, a substantial jump. This suggests buyer caution.

7. Finally, McKinsey published a review online which suggests that – a) B2B customers are open to choosing different self-serve and digital channels, b) that the move to digital channels continues and c) that there seems to be a solidity to the use of these remote, digital channels.

The lesson. Reviewing all the above combined, there are some conclusions to be made; volume and low-level selling will move faster towards digital channels, the world of selling will simply not remain the same, the historic and critical need to differentiate yourself will only increase, the admin overhead in enterprise sales will likely increase. So, embrace change, look for value messages, operate as efficiently as you can in the new world.

Notes

_____

_____

_____

_____

_____

_____

_____

_____

_____

_____

_____

_____

_____

_____

_____

_____

_____

_____

_____

_____

_____

Chapter 20

Why we Need to Professionalise Sales

By Andrew Hough

"Being professional is just clearly the way to go and helps you on the road to longevity."

Amanda Seyfried

Imagine you are at a party and are asked what you do. I doubt there are many salespeople in Britain who have not been subjected to a remark about Del Boy or Arthur Daley when they say they are in sales. This is not a flattering association. Del Boy and Arthur, supposedly the archetypal salesmen, are notorious for cutting corners, ducking, and diving, making a fast buck and generally selling people what they don't need. Lies, greed and cheating, in other words. They may be legendary comic characters, but they are the polar opposite of professional. And if, at this same party, you were to say that salespeople don't deserve their bad reputation and need to be regarded in the same light as doctors and pilots, your remark would raise eyebrows and probably cause some laughter.

For a profession that employs nearly 12% of the UK workforce and keeps the economy turning (because, as we should never tire of repeating, nothing happens in business until something is sold), sales is certainly not viewed with the respect it deserves - not even in the business world. Selling is as important to business as marketing and accounting and continues to grow massively in complexity and in the amount of skill and responsibility it entails. But while employers respect marketing and accounting as professions without question and take their nationally recognised qualifications and membership of their professional bodies into account when recruiting, in too many quarters sales is seen as a lesser thing - almost a con trick. Respect for salespeople is missing.

The way many salespeople are treated by their employers and viewed by their customers is about as far away from parity with other professional people in business as it is possible to get. Salespeople are not even paid the same way as marketeers and finance officers, who are given a regular salary. Like the dogs in the yard, salespeople are kept hungry with the incentive of a juicy bone waved in their faces; they are set monthly targets to hit. Let's leave aside the issue of whether this form of motivation encourages the best behaviour in salespeople (it doesn't). The bigger problem is that, thanks to the widespread habit of over-quota'ing, each month 67% of salespeople find their 'number' proves too high to meet. Month after month, salespeople are set up to fail, and take home less than their on-target earnings.

Treating salespeople in this way is dispiriting and counterproductive. No wonder, then, that the average tenure in a sales role continues to sink. In the IT sector, the average length of stay in an inside sales job is currently less than two years, costing businesses thousands in lost productivity while they expensively onboard new staff. No wonder, too, that business leaders are experiencing ever-increasing difficulties in recruiting effective salespeople. Inevitably, the shortage of good salespeople is negatively affecting business performance. Month after month, year after year, the UK economy is suffering incrementally because we have failed to find the right approach towards sales and sellers.

A sea change is needed

As I am the founder and CEO of an international body called the Institute of Sales Professionals, you can guess where my argument is going. I passionately believe that professionalising sales is the way ahead. Recent events have made change even more essential, if organisations are to cope with the speed at which doing business is transforming. During Covid and Brexit, salespeople have been obliged to acquire the technical skills to sell through the omnichannel while acting as consultants and influencers, and expanding their knowledge of logistics, law and finance. It's simply time to recognise this: selling, and above all B2B selling, is a professional job that requires professional skills. We need to bring salespeople into parity with other business disciplines. Selling should no longer be a dead-end occupation in which talented youngsters circle from employer to employer then drift away and are lost to the industry. Sales has been left behind. It's now time for it to catch up.

Change will begin once the profession agrees a body of fundamental knowledge, skills and behaviours that salespeople need. Having a wide range of knowledge and skills at their fingertips on which to draw is the first level of professionalism. When they encounter a client for the first time, a salesperson should be able to select from among the many selling methods the style that is most appropriate for the customer: solutions selling, the consultative approach and so on. At present, even identifying the best salespeople to recruit is a lottery, especially for SMEs. This is likely to remain the case until the nationwide system of apprenticeships and qualifications in professional selling set up by the Institute of Sales Professionals (ISP) becomes more widely adopted and recognised. Accredited by Ofsted, and with every training standard from school-leaver to postgraduate degree-level based round the same fundamental competency framework, these can help employers to differentiate between sellers with differing levels of skill, and to have confidence in whom they are taking on.

Many more employers need to start treating young sales recruits the same way as they would young finance officers: as professional people, not just as a means for the sales manager to meet their number. Salespeople should be able to expect the opportunity to increase their skill, experience, and rewards as they gain seniority, and be given support to progress. Looking back over my own varied experience of managers as I learned my trade, the next stage of professionalism involves defining the culture of leadership. Let's get away from the focus on just the number in compensation packages: employers should also be testing attitude and ethical stance when considering rewards. If the seller is given the choice of the right or wrong path, will they take the right one? Employers need to ensure their salespeople are on a ladder of continual professional development, punctuated by qualifications for those that want them, so that they can progress in their career. The ISP has a famously tough ethics exam, which individual members are encouraged to sit: many employers put their whole sales team through it. It also offers a CPD programme which can be tailored to employers' needs.

The next generation of sellers

We need to change our attitude to sales development and look to sport and even aviation for how these professions implement deliberate learning against skills, reinforced by practice. The model we need is similar to how an athlete improves, spending hours with their coach examining their technique, practising and improving it. Pilots have a culture of reporting and talking through any adverse incidents so lessons can be learned. Salespeople too need to be coached for success, and to learn from mistakes. Any sales leaders reading this article should talk to the ISP about how they can set up a professional culture of sales in their organisation, backed by a professional body.

Helping young salespeople to progress is a cause close to my heart. The ISP has set up its Emerging Professionals Network (EPN) to nurture talent. The EPN provides peer support and mentoring to help young sellers excel and to open their eyes to the joys of selling. I am sure that many readers, like me, have found sales to be a fantastic career, full of interest and reward. I am equally sure that many of you, like me, fell into it by accident. In my final year at university, I was determined to go into management and was quite surprised to discover at Barclays Mercantile that the activity that gave me the most satisfaction was being given a territory, a target and wide discretion on how to meet it, with the backing of a big brand. Passion for the job is for me the next essential quality of professionalism, an underlying commitment to selling. We need salespeople who want to work in sales their whole career. We need to instill pride in the profession. For this, we ourselves as managers need to model pride in selling.

Gaining recognition

It is only by putting all this into place that we can get to the stage where people outside the industry start to recognise sales as a profession. Only then can we get to a situation where school-leavers and graduates are deliberately choosing sales as a career, rather than reluctantly or accidentally falling into it. Only then, perhaps, will the references to Del Boy start to slacken off.

So far, I have barely mentioned one of the most important reasons for professionalising sales: and that is the positive impact on the client. As a young salesperson I enjoyed discovering that the important thing wasn't the product itself, but what it could do for the customer. If I sold a loan, for example, it had to arrive quickly enough to be of use. Good selling ensures the customer gets the product they need, but professional selling is about co-creating a solution that makes the customer's business stronger into the future. And of course, professional selling increases the turnover of the seller's organisation too. It creates a win:win that boosts profits, productivity and morale on both sides of the deal.

Spread out across the entire UK economy, imagine what a difference more professional sales practices could bring. The former Bank of England chief economist Andy Haldane has said that just a 1% increase in productivity in Britain's long tail of underperforming businesses would add tens of billions to national turnover. It is not hard to imagine that becoming a reality – if salespeople had the professional skills to steer more deals over the line, and to qualify out of negotiations liable to end in no decision. Think of the reputational benefits abroad, too, for the country that was the first to embrace professional standards in selling. Think how it could enhance its reputation as the country to do business if its salespeople were ambassadors for the whole country. Imagine how trade with the wider world could thrive.

About the author

Andrew Hough is CEO of the Institute for Sales Professionals, the professional membership body for the sales industry in the UK and worldwide, which is a force for positive change within the profession. The ISP was formed from the merger of the Association of Professional Sales (APS) which Andy founded, with the Institute of Sales Management. Before founding the APS, Andy had a long career in sales leadership, latterly as Vice President (Enterprise and Mid-Range Storage) at EMC. The ISP's mission is to create a world where sales is recognised and celebrated as a respected profession, through chartership, qualifications and exacting standards. To join the ISP or find out more, visit www.the-isp.org or contact membership services at enquiries@the-isp.org.

Notes

_____

_____

_____

_____

_____

_____

_____

_____

_____

_____

_____

_____

_____

_____

_____

_____

_____

_____

_____

_____

_____

_____

Chapter

21

Honesty – the Best Policy?

By Peter Houghton

"I believe fundamental honesty is the keystone of business."

Harvey S Firestone

As I look back at my working life, I have spent 35+ years in purchasing roles and then the final five in sales. An interesting combination, and a real contrast! The 35 years in purchasing was all in Motorsport. Of course, to the outsider, this might sound and look glamorous, but for most of the team the work is done, like other jobs, in the office or factory. Even the members of the team going to each event will tell you that they see an airport, a hotel, and a circuit and they all look remarkably similar all over the world. However, everyone has a passion for what they are doing, and one gets to see the results of your efforts, good or bad, very quickly. In this environment, what were my procurement priorities?

Motorsport is, of course, seriously leading edge. Since the development of parts is very rapid, it is important that the correct balance between Quality, Cost and Delivery is achieved.

Since the failure of a part purchased can result in actual, not just potentially, fatal consequences, one must ensure that high Quality is a given.

In this fast-moving world, Delivery is generally the next priority - the parts being needed exactly on time, and even a day late might mean the part will no longer be required and could in the worst event mean that a complete up-date package for the team misses an event.

The final element is Cost and despite Motorsport having an image that suggests money is no object, budgets still exist and if all is spent, development would have to stop. Balancing these three or better said two, since one is mandatory (quality), it was always necessary to develop a strong feeling of trust between us and the supplier and when that existed one could be certain that the relationship would flourish. But isn't it interesting that, I, as a buyer, typically saw cost as the least critical of my three priorities? This is often the case inside an organisation, though I have seen salespeople so often focus on giving the buyer the 'best price' as if, in some way, that is always the highest priority!

I still remember an incident from sometime back which was not regarding one of these mission-critical and highly technical parts, but was from the "mundane" area of office supplies. It was only a matter of the supply of a particular sort of paper. This was when continuous multi-layer paper (fed through a tractor drive on the printer) was commonplace and we had been using three-layer paper (with copies going to various departments) and decided that four-layer was now needed. The first rep we contacted, visited us to discuss the matter, but then said that while he could supply what we wanted he would prefer not to do so, because he was certain that we would have problems using it. The second rep visited and immediately quoted to supply. We ordered, all was delivered and, lo and behold, we then had problems with our regular multi-layer paper 'salads'. A really bad buying experience.

Not long after this, the team was growing in numbers, and we started to bring a bit more structure within the purchase systems. One of the first areas to be reviewed was office materials, where we decided to work through a much more detailed framework contract. After the initial groundwork we were down to a choice of two suppliers, and there was nothing really to say which was better. Both could do the job, both had good reputations, both could deliver. However, one of the choices was the firm whose rep had told us that we would have problems with what we were insisting on buying previously. Remembering his honest response and ethical approach and the fact that he had lost any commission by saying 'no' to supplying what we were insisting upon, we decided to go with that firm since we felt we really could trust them. Since our team size then grew from only double figures of personnel to four figure numbers over the next few years and we were still using that supplier for everything, I am sure the long-term benefits to that company and commission to the rep 'more than covered' the slight loss caused by his honesty earlier.

And here is the lesson for everyone in sales. Buyers notice your behaviour. I have seen buyers test salespeople by asking for something that they already know will not work. How does the salesperson respond? That salesperson will probably not even know they have just been tested! But, even putting that to one side, in the long term, being honest makes your life simpler, you sleep better AND your revenues will also grow over time. Reputation is just so important. And what about the flip side? If you and/or your company gain a reputation for being a bit 'fast' or overly aggressive to sell whatever the cost, do you really think that will help you in the medium to long term? We all know the answer to that one, don't we! And once you have a poor reputation, does selling get easier or harder? How hard is it to shake off a reputation like that? Make your life easier, just don't go there.

I know, wearing my other career hat, just how much pressure there is to get the sale, even when you are not the right solution. Take a moment to think about what happens if you do close a deal this way. Is your customer happy? Will they recommend you? Do you have less or more work as they try to use your solution/product/offering?

And finally, if your employer is pushing you to sell unethically, what do you do? I would suggest that you push back, based on the above arguments, common sense and logic. If they still force you, well then, you have a choice to make, don't you? Honesty and ethics create competitive advantage!

Peter Houghton is now enjoying 'nearly full' retirement. Its only 'nearly full' since he could not resist saying 'Yes' when two old colleagues asked if he would give some part time help to their new venture. Peter now looks back on nearly five decades of working life, which started at 16 as an apprentice at Ford, later moving with family to Germany and staying 29 years with Toyota Motorsport and finishing with the last five years spent in sales for a precision machining company. He says – *"I can honestly agree with Frank Sinatra – Regrets I've had a few, but then again too few to mention".*

Notes

_____

_____

_____

_____

_____

_____

_____

_____

_____

_____

_____

_____

_____

_____

_____

_____

_____

_____

_____

_____

_____

_____

_____

Chapter 22

The DMU

By Jim Irving

"Great things in business are never done by one person. They're done by a team of people."

Steve Jobs

Many years ago (in the late 1980's to be a bit more precise), I studied for and gained an MBA. My specialism was 'International Marketing'. Most of what I learned has, to be honest, withered away over time. However, a few thoughts and concepts are as clear today as they were for me when I first heard them.

One of those is the incredible story, told by a lecturer to help us students better understand priorities. This is covered in both of my earlier books so will not feature again here. Another is the concept of the DMU. It hit me like a punch when I heard it (I was selling 'big tin' at the time, and it instantly explained several losses I had recently suffered). I think the DMU is so simple, and yet so profound for all who sell B2B at any level.

So, what is this 'DMU'?

Philip Kotler, sometimes referred to as 'The Godfather of Modern Marketing', introduced the concept in around 2004 – or possibly even earlier. DMU stands for 'Decision Making Unit' – and it is dynamite for sales as well as marketing. He defined the DMU as *"all individuals and groups that take part in the decision-making process relating to the negotiation of products /services".* That seems like a very simple thing, doesn't it? But it can deliver power and advantage to you as you fight for business.

Put simply, it is the sum of all the people who will have a voice in the decision to buy (or not to buy) your service, product or solution. Why is it so important?

Human nature always leads us to the easier path, like water running downhill. That means that all too often, as we sell complex solutions or services to large organisations, salespeople focus on a friendly contact or even just their first contact. It's a big temptation, and very easy to do - but so risky and wrong.

The DMU is the sum of all those people who can and might influence and/or decide on your deal - users, technical specialists like IT, Finance and Procurement, the sponsor, the budget holder, the final decision maker, your coach etc.

And why do I include it specifically in this book? Well, I have experienced, and research has now proven, a developing trend among corporate companies – those people you want to sell to.

In chapter 19, I mentioned the recent Gartner survey. They found that for important corporate purchases, the average number of people involved in the decision had risen from 5.4 to 6.8 in just two years! Ask yourself, how many people are you speaking to? The risks around missing some of those who are involved are enormous - especially if your competitor is reaching out to them.

Just imagine you are selling to an organisation. You have found your friendly contact and you are getting on well. At the end of the buying process there will – most often – be a session in a meeting room to make their purchase decision. All in there have a voice, maybe some much more than others, but still there are multiple different views and feelings. If you have been working with one, or even two of those players (let's take Gartner's number and say there are seven in total) and your competition have reached six, how do you think that conversation is likely to go? What are the odds of you winning? Now turn that around! If you have reached six and sold well and your competition are typical salespeople and have only spoken to one or two now what do your chances look like? Even just the act of reaching out more broadly will start to make individuals think better of you.

This is the world of political and enterprise selling. Those who understand it almost always win.

How does Kotler categorise all these different contributors? Here is his naming convention for them –

- **The initiator.** Whose idea was this procurement? Who is championing the process?
- **The decider.** When everyone gathers in that room and the conversation concludes, who do they all look to for 'the nod'?
- **The gatekeeper(s).** This group can range from admin staff, to PAs, to project managers and those assigned to 'have a look at the market and report back'.
- **Users.** Who must make your service, product, or solution work internally, to have this project succeed?
- **Influencers.** Those who have a view, perhaps some specialist expertise, but are not directly involved in the final decision. They influence, but don't decide. In technology buying, for example, perhaps a department owns the budget and is making the purchase. But I would bet that their IT department will have an opinion on which offering might fit best with their core, central systems.
- **Buyers.** These are the professional buyers, usually assigned to such projects. Typically, they will be procurement professionals.

Think of your biggest current opportunity? How many of those groups or individuals are you reaching? Who's missing from that list?

But that's not all...

Kotler's point was two-fold. First, that these people exist, and they all have a voice. But, even more important, that they all view the situation differently. They all have different wins. Once you start to consider this, it's not rocket science. If you want, you can ignore Kotler's categories, but then ask yourself in your own terms, exactly who will have any voice in my prospect's purchase decision? Have I met them yet? And most important, what would they be looking for? Let's consider a few job titles that would normally be involved in a big decision to show what I mean –

Users – ease of use, simplicity
FD – overall financial picture. What does your solution do to help the company numbers?
CEO and head of Sales - how can you help growth?
Procurement – best value and/or lowest price
Influencers – they will want their feelings/position listened to and considered

Never try to lump them all in with a single sales message. The art of winning big deals is all about delivering value to each person - and its frequently very different value.

A single message will not hit all their buttons. It's that simple. So, THINK when you are heading into calls or meetings. What is their 'win'? What is their language and approach? Then adapt. The best salespeople always mould, adapt and tune their message to their audience.

The lesson. Selling into complex organisations is complex! Never make the mistake of taking the easy path and hoping it's simpler than it really is!

Notes

_____

_____

_____

_____

_____

_____

_____

_____

_____

_____

_____

_____

_____

_____

_____

_____

_____

_____

_____

_____

_____

Chapter

23

Lazy Pigeons

By Jeremy Jacobs

"One key to success is demanding more than adequacy, never settling for good enough and always doing a little bit more."

Michael Josephson

Chaim Perez was a very dour individual. Slight-framed with a sallow complexion, he rarely smiled as he got on with his job – as manager of the community laundry – easy enough when all the machinery was working. He was competent, efficient and barked out instructions to those who had the dubious pleasure of working with him. Born of Eastern European émigré parents in the Paraguayan capital, Asuncion, Chaim decided to make his life as a long-term volunteer in Israel after the Six-Day War in 1967. Doing the whole kibbutz schtick was a rite of passage for young men like him and for the many thousands of volunteers from all over the world who followed over the next few decades, including me but for less than a year.

The daily ritual of working in the laundry started at five thirty in the morning. A quick shower and then off to work which was a pleasant three-minute walk away. Work began at six. Two of hours of toil later, one would be allowed out for breakfast in the communal hall, then back to work at 9 before finishing around ten thirty.

I put up with this schedule for about a week. It was patently obvious to me that I could do the first two hours work in just over an hour if one worked efficiently. Chaim agreed with my plan and so I had an hour's break for breakfast (including twenty minutes listening to the BBC World Service) before resuming my duties. The working day now finished at ten in the morning. What a delight! So, what to make of all this? Was I being efficient, effective or just plain lazy? Some of you might think a blend of all three.

The vast majority of the public will have enjoyed taking a walk through a public park or country estate. Occasionally, the perambulation is interrupted by a band of feral pigeons – in a Woody Allen film, they were referred to as "rats with wings" - who seem intent on blocking one's path. Usually, if you walk tentatively through them they will flap their wings and waddle off out of your and harm's way. Sometimes they will fly away but more often than not they don't. Flight takes great effort, both mentally and physically, so the pigeons opt for the easy solution.

The same could be said for sales activity of any type. Many budding and even experienced salespeople just do enough to ensure that quota whether of revenue, discovery calls or presentations is met. These tend to be the sales guys who bunk off early, don't gen up on their industry knowledge and fail to find enough time to plan or brush up their sales skills. High flyers seem to achieve more but the average guys, the also-rans and the downright lazy so-and-so's just don't go the extra mile. The main reason may be down to a phenomenon called the L.E.P. or Least Effort Principle, sometimes referred to as the principle of least effort. It was first discovered by the French philosopher Guillame Ferrero in 1894. L.E.P. is a theory which suggests that us humans are wired up to carry out tasks with the least effort, or to choose the path of least resistance or effort. But in the sales industry, one can't afford to be lazy. Mark McCormack, author of "What They Don't Teach You at Harvard Business School" and a master planner, suggested that to make it in sales – or any other field for that matter - you have to work late, work hard and work smart.

A sister of LEP is the Status Quo Bias. It is one of over one-hundred and fifty currently recognised cognitive biases. The Status Quo Bias comes at you when you hear those fateful words as a territory salesperson from your prospect – *"we've just bought one"* or *"we don't like your brand"*. When involved with more complex B2B sales situations, you will often read an e-mail or letter with something like this; "the board has met and has decided that we cannot continue with the project you've kindly put forward" followed by a list of 'reasons' – some genuine, many aren't. You could just shrug your shoulders and say to yourself the old 1990's sales maxim *"all buyers are liars",* but you should really just consider it as another manifestation of the Status Quo Bias. Behavioural scientists would describe the Status Quo Bias as being 'if it ain't broke, don't fix it'.

After all, sticking with what you know is safer, easier, and as we've learnt it doesn't require any effort.

So, what are these cognitive biases? A quick trawl on Google will give you this answer: Cognitive or thinking biases **result from the way in which we process information** - most of it by using something known as System 1 thinking. This was developed by psychologist Daniel Kahneman who postulated that decision-making is not entirely based on conscious, rational thought. In his International Bestseller book *Thinking Fast and Slow*, Kahneman highlights two separate types of thinking: "System 1" is knee-jerk, driven by instinct and previous learning; "System 2" on the other hand is slower, driven by logic and reasoning. Even when we believe we are making decisions based on rational considerations, our System 1 beliefs, biases, and intuition drive many of our choices and especially those of our company buyers! Cognitive biases go hand in hand with the field of Behavioural Science or BS for short. Behavioural Science as described by behavioural science guru Richard Shotton is how people behave rather than how they think they behave.

Daniel Kahneman along with Amos Tversky also put forward the notion that Prospect Theory (this gave Kahneman the Nobel Prize for Psychology), or as it's more commonly known, Loss Aversion Theory, is connected with the Status Quo Bias. Most buyers make the status quo from their perspective and tend to view any change from the status quo as a loss. People tend to view losses more than any economic or efficiency gain. The key here is for salespeople to frame their sales proposal in such a way that it becomes less of a risk than the customer's status quo.

So how can salespeople overcome the Status Quo Bias?

According to Tim Reisterer of Corporate Visions, one method is to explain to your customer that they have 'unconsidered needs' – you will have done your research first! An unconsidered need could be something your customer under appreciates or a solution that they aren't even aware of. Then, you must explain the cost of doing nothing v the cost of acquisition. Finally, explain in a clear and concise way the contrast between the customers current state and a future scenario.

Jeremy Jacobs is The Sales Rainmaker. He has devoted his life to understanding sales issues. He continues to research and share evolving as well as new insights into sales interactions. Unlike many of the profession who continue to preach out-of-date systems (methods) from the 1980s and 1990s he looks to the future. The way we buy and sell has undergone a radical shift in expectations and behaviours. What used to work often now seems hackneyed and artificial. Jeremy gets to the heart of current issues with his mentoring and shows clients and customers a better, more sustainable way to engage. The digital age, with new brain science, makes the old techniques appear false and forced.

He is London-based and can be reached on:
T: +44 (0) 7778 035735
E: jj@thesalesrainmaker.co.uk

Notes

_____

_____

_____

_____

_____

_____

_____

_____

_____

_____

_____

_____

_____

_____

_____

_____

_____

_____

_____

_____

_____

Chapter

24

14 Powerful LinkedIn Tips

By Niraj Kapur

"Proactive people focus their efforts on things they can do something about. The nature of their energy is positive."

Stephen Covey

LinkedIn needs to be part of your sales strategy.

756 million users can't be wrong.

Here's some more amazing stats about LinkedIn -

90% of people do nothing. They don't scroll, they don't engage, and they miss out on so much business.

7% like and comment on people's posts. This is good for your visibility and good for the person who's post you're commenting on.

3% post content. This is where you get LinkedIn enquiries and business generated.

Most people haven't been trained properly or regularly in sales, which is why most people can't sell.

LinkedIn is no different. Most people haven't invested in a LinkedIn trainer and are not generating the results they're capable of.

Don't be ashamed of selling, it's the foundation of your business.

Businesses don't fail because people are lazy, most business owners work hard.

Businesses don't fail because people are stupid, every business owner has different smarts.

They fail due to lack of sales.

Clients ask how long it takes before they get business on LinkedIn.

Some people take 6 months. Others take 6 weeks.

So, here's 14 tips for LinkedIn that will help you generate more sales:

1. Have A Headline Banner
People are inundated all day with adverts and noise from every social media app and platform. So, you need to stand out. Have a Headline banner that tells people how you help them or shows people that what you do makes a difference. Don't leave it blank.

2. About Section
This is where most people go wrong. They only write a few lines, or they cram it full of text.

Tell people how you help them, the clients you serve, why you do what you do and have a paragraph at the end that talks about your hobbies. It humanises the person behind the business.

3. Recommendations Matter
According to Nielsen, 92% of people will trust a testimonial from a peer and 72% trust a testimonial from a stranger. People who say you've done great work makes the business process easier and quicker. People don't buy your product, they buy outcomes/results/ROI. You're missing out without testimonials on your website and LinkedIn recommendations.

4. Post Consistently
So many people want the magic dust and I understand why. Telling someone they can lose weight by eating what they want is way more attractive than saying it will take months of pain, sweat, heartache and cravings to overcome your diet.

My job as a coach is to get you results, not give you the easy options.

Posting once a week or once in a while never builds momentum. Start posting twice a week, then three times a week and keep building to 4-5 times a week if possible.

5. Like and Comment on Other Peoples Posts

This helps you be seen and supports the other person as well. So, it's a win-win. When you comment, have 5 words of more. It's good for the LinkedIn algorithm. Saying "yes" or "awesome" has no effect.

6. Don't Sell as Soon as You Connect

Nobody wants to be sold to; however, they do want to buy. Relationships first, selling second.

7. Tagging

If you are thanking someone, appreciating an author, had someone train you or do something nice, then tagging them on LinkedIn is generous and says a lot about you. Don't tag people if you don't know them or for the sake of boosting your product or service. You can get blocked very quickly.

8. Kindness Matters

Kindness and patience cost nothing, yet they're worth so much. If you see someone struggling for a job, help them out. If someone is going through a tough time, message and ask how they are. Help people with whatever skills you can offer. Some will appreciate it. Some will surprisingly never say thank you. It doesn't matter. Always do the right thing when nobody is looking. LinkedIn isn't just a business network, it's a people network. I get more business because I'm a decent kind human being than I do being a LinkedIn expert. People vastly underestimate the importance of giving and caring.

9. Quality

The quality of your connections is more important than the numbers. There are people with 25,000 followers that get nothing and people with less than 2,000 followers who get business monthly.

10. Personal Stories

There's been a shift on LinkedIn since March 2020 lockdown to sharing more personal stories and being kind. Kindness is a superpower and people buy people – so don't be afraid of telling your story. Having a personal post once a week helped people connect with you. You don't have to showcase pictures of your children and dogs, although that does help, and it performs especially well on a Sunday.

11. Do Your Research

Read someone's website for news/blogs/case studies and see what you can talk about from that. Look at their LinkedIn profile and see what you have in common. It makes you stand out from the crowd.

12. Use Voice Notes

LinkedIn voice notes are an effective way to communicate especially if you're an introvert. Go to the LinkedIn mobile app, select "message" and instead of typing a message, hold down the microphone icon and speak. When finished, you can cancel and start again or press "send."

I send birthday messages by voice notes and long messages because it saves time - plus your energy and tone come across well on voice notes.

13. Embrace Video

Video is the way forward. It has been for 6 months and will be in the future. Shoot a 20-30 second video and send it through LinkedIn messenger. My clients get 40% conversation on video prospecting, much higher than cold email 1%, phone 0.5% or email to existing clients 25%.

Again, your personality comes across in a way that text and email never will. This is also wonderful for clients that have gone cold. It shows you have made a massive effort that the competition is not making.

14. Enjoy The Process

As the great Tony Robbins said when I attended his 4-day 'Unleash The Power Within' event, *"the key to success is progress."* Business is a marathon, not a sprint. So is LinkedIn.

Niraj Kapur is a trusted sales coach, LinkedIn Trainer and author of the Amazon bestsellers, Everybody Works in Sales and The Easy Guide to Sales for Business Owners. In April 2021, he was nominated by Salesforce as a Top Sales Influencer to Follow in 2021.
He's generated results for over 300 clients. To achieve more, check out **www.everybodyworksinsales.com** or **https://uk.linkedin.com/in/nkapur**

Notes

Chapter

25

10 Reasons You're Not Selling – and How to Fix Them

By Steve Knapp

"Being a professional...is making fewer mistakes than others, as few as possible."

Francoise Giroud

In my own experience and, through my training work at PLAN.GROW.DO, I see ten issues all the time. This chapter focuses on first describing them, and then how best to overcome them. They are not listed in any priority form; they are all equally impactful on your potential success.

So, without any further ado...

1. You talk too much, worse you don't listen
You've caught the verbal's... question after question.
No well thought out questions, just spray and pray.
You are looking for your poor prospect to submit!

The fix to this is you! Your goal is to talk for a maximum of 30% of the meeting. But how? You'll achieve this by preparing great questions. Ask them and then listen. Don't think about your next question, really listen. If you're dialling in, then record it. If its Face-to-face reflect as soon as you get back in the car.

2. You don't prepare for your Customer Sales Meetings
Do you deserve to succeed? Do you not value your time, your clients time? Of course you do, so why do you act so unprofessionally?

It's simple. Use a pre call plan to ensure you give your prospect the space to talk, that you keep control and that don't waste time. Guess what, you'll get better sales outcomes, and you'll look professional.

3. You don't write down what happened before
You're happy to go over previously trodden ground and go back into those verbal's... are you surprised you aren't closing deals?

Maybe you feel it's time to roll your eyes, but write things down! Focus on recording and then confirming the points you're noting during and at the end of your meeting, then follow up with an email if appropriate. Being clear on any next steps, who's doing what and where you are in the sales process is basic stuff, but so often not done.

4. You ask for the order far too early
You're not following a sales process so how do you know where the sale is up to? You're asking for the business when your prospect is still analysing their options. You are working to your 'Sales Time' not in their 'Buying Time'.

Here's what's happening. The seller is moving through a sales process, but it doesn't match your buyers buying journey. When it goes wrong it's because you are running separate races. Your first goal is to make sure you are both in the same place – and then keep it there as you proceed. Follow this sales process which I use daily - SPANCOP (Suspect, Prospect, Analyse, Negotiate, Close, Order, Pay).

While you are doing this, your buyers' journey is also underway. It looks like this - Unaware, Aware, Consider, Decision.

5. Your offer isn't as good as you think it is
You've become lazy. You haven't bothered to keep your offer current, and your solutions are so yesterday. Your buyer sees you as irrelevant.

It's time to research. Profile your ideal client and work out the problems they have that you can solve, what opportunities you can create for them and how you can help them look good in their business. Also analyse your overall market dynamics – growing, shrinking, needs innovation, your solution fit to their needs?
(don't underestimate this one).

6. You don't differentiate from your competition
I love to win business from businesses like yours. The game in town is to be different, to have something you stand for and to shout about it. You're making it easy for me!

We call this being a Leading Voice. Note, not the Loudest Voice or an Annoying Voice!

The game in town in B2B sales is to have something you stand for, something your buyer will recognise you for and value. It might be championing your sector in some way. Take time to work out your messaging and to shout about it.

From here you create content, attend events, speak and all the time you're differentiating.

7. You have become tired and boring
I mean look at you! When was the last time that website, brochure, presentation was refreshed?

Just think about how you do or do not put your ideal customer at the centre of all your content, your digital assets, or your sales tools?

If you are not constantly looking to improve your content, make it exciting and relevant then guess what? If your prospect stumbles on your stuff they will quickly close it, delete it, or scroll on – boring!

Please don't tell me you have a fax number or a Google+ on your sales collateral!

8. You're happy to focus on price
You're taking the easy road. Selling on price is easy. You avoid value selling because that's harder. You must know your sector or segment and product.

Price will matter at some point; we can't put our head in the sand. Sales experts broadcasting "sell value". You know what, you can sell value and your prospect will still say "how much"?

My view, you should "build value" and when the time is right to talk price it will be a far more incidental part of the process. How you deliver the promised value will be far more important to them.

You need to understand how your offer adds a value over and above competition so you can charge what you want to charge.

9. You don't offer a logical next step
Sometimes you forget to sell and that's one of the reasons you don't sell! You haven't even considered where to send your prospect next to keep them in your eco system.

This is where modern selling and marketing work like hand in glove. You should map out your buyers' journey and have content that helps them in their buying journey.

Consider the Unaware phase (see above), your contents purpose here is solely to make people Aware of you.

Therefore, your logical next step isn't "buy my stuff". Your logical next step could be "read more here" or "sign up to this webinar".

In both cases you will be building value by adding insight and not just information.

Offering a next logical step is missed by many and guess what happens if your prospect is not guided?

Yep, you've got it...the competition gets a nice warm prospect.

10. You don't know where your clients hang out
You've not dusted down your networking plan for years and all you do is see your mates...and business talk, well you all know each other don't you – doh!

The solution here is to step back and have a strategy that connects you to the right people or at least one that gets you seen in the eco system of the people that need to know who you are and what you do.

Where do they hang out? And remember this is not just in a traditional physical sense but B2B selling is very lively over at LinkedIn and in Facebook Groups. Oh, and I should mention, don't turn down the opportunity to speak and stand out from the crowd (check out point 6).

So those are my top 10 areas for you to consider. I am sure you are strong in some of them, but hopefully this chapter has been a timely reminder on the others!

Steve Knapp's inspirational selling techniques are still the cornerstone of Shell International. He rose through the ranks to become responsible for the success of the company's sales teams right across the globe.

Steve's now using that incredible knowledge to help business owners and salespeople embrace a modern selling approach.

The author of Funnel Vision - Selling Made Easy, Steve provides sales training in energetic, pragmatic, actionable and outcome focused lessons that stick and deliver results.

Find Steve here:
www.linkedin.com/in/steveknappsales

Contact him here:
E: steve@plangrowdo.com

Notes

_____

_____

_____

_____

_____

_____

_____

_____

_____

_____

_____

_____

_____

_____

_____

_____

_____

_____

_____

Chapter

26

The Often-Overlooked Impressions That Make the Biggest Impact

By Jonathan Lancaster

"Anything with your name should leave a lasting impression!"

Marcia Brown

And you might think I mean schmoozing clients over lunch, polite conversation on Zoom, or a firm handshake (or touching of elbows). Which, by the way, can be important. But that's not what I'm here to write about. I'm here to write about all the hidden, thus often-overlooked impressions you make with a prospect or active client that have the biggest impact on your performance and results.

And, yes, those impressions start from the very first contact with a prospect, during a competitive bid, and beyond.

Why do they matter?
We all want our clients to see us as trusted "strategic" advisors and partners.

Why? Because we know it means we can build more valuable – and profitable – client relationships that lead to repeat business, case studies, and referrals.

But with mounting pressure to perform and deliver results in less time, we can overlook what really matters, to stand out in the ever more competitive and increasingly digital environment.

So, what often-overlooked impressions drive superior performance and results?

Like many, my first taste of sales was selling door-to-door. That was in the early noughties. I then found myself in enterprise software sales and then consulting. I now help firms build quality sales pipelines, win competitive deals, and grow more valuable contracts.

I advise, and I teach, but above all, I practice what I preach.

From that experience, here is what I have found to be the impressions that matter.

I have put these together into a simple model for you called EDGE.

The EDGE Model

EDGE focuses on the four vital performance elements of **Engage, Discover, Grow** and **Execute**.

First and foremost, firms that consistently outperform their rivals do so because there is a solid connection and even greater alignment between their business strategy and culture.

They clearly understand their culture and strategy and how – when both are understood and continuously worked on – they can build a competitive edge in their market.

The topics of culture and strategy are beyond the scope of this short chapter. Thus, I signpost you to some additional resources throughout, should you wish to explore in more depth.

(E) Engage – around a shared approach to client-facing sales practice

First, there is a commitment to ethical and professional sales practice across the business. That commitment to professionalism in sales is, of course, set by the "tone at the top" with leadership. It runs like a golden thread with everyone that engages and serves prospects and clients.

That involves some work to identify the personal and collective values, attitudes, and behaviours that serve your business strategy. Thus, everyone who engages with prospects and clients does so in a way consistent with what the business stands for and what it wants to achieve.

An example of a cultural value and behaviour some firms might want to display in every client engagement is *teamwork*. In their two bestselling books, The Challenger Sale and The Challenger Customer, the authors discover that sellers who engage in competitive deals as a team effort outperformed those that did not.

To identify your personal values and how these influence your decisions and actions, a leading culture consultancy – NDC – gives you (as a purchaser of this book) – complimentary access to their Personal Values Assessment tool. **https://bit.ly/ndc-pva** On completion, you will receive a report and worksheet by email. You can also ask colleagues to take the assessment too and compare results to learn more about each other.

(D) – Discover

High-performing sales teams are equipped with the capabilities to discover and anticipate client needs and opportunities earlier. They have moved from a 'reactive' transactional relationship to a 'proactive' strategic partnership with clients.

A series of impressions make up the 'Discover' element. The most impactful is to create value for your prospects and clients much earlier in their buying journey. And quite often, that happens well before they are even considering options to the business problem you might be able to solve.

So, to do that, here are some steps that have proven successful:

I. **Become laser focused on your target.** Rather than serving anyone and everyone, you build specialist knowledge around a client's profile and the sector you want to help. Thus, you learn to speak their language. That might involve partnering with marketing and other colleagues. Still, ultimately you will lead a pursuit plan that positions you as someone worth having a discovery conversation with. You are a specialist who brings unique perspectives, insights and ideas to a business challenge or problem your clients might have.

II. Have a legitimate reason to engage. To stand out from other sellers competing for your client's attention, have a legitimate reason to engage (whether by phone, email, message etc.). That involves some quick research you have done about their organisation. It could be that you have noticed in an industry publication that they have plans for growth through mergers or acquisitions. Or you might see from their Annual Review that they have several business goals you believe you might be able to help them achieve. Whatever it is, take the time to care because your prospect is more likely to take notice and the time to engage with you. Of course, scheduled prospecting outreach requires some professional persistence! And be creative with your communication channels.

III. Come prepared for each engagement. Whether a first meeting or a follow-up, how will you create value from the encounter? What is the purpose of the discussion from the client's perspective? And what are your 2 – 3 objectives for the meeting? How will the time be spent? Will you collaborate with all attendees on the agenda? What valuable discovery questions will you ask? And how will you define a successful meeting? We can all get better at our discussions, and these questions help prepare for that.

(G) – Grow

Firms that outperform their rivals have a culture of coaching and continuous improvement, which means that everyone can grow and perform at their best.

Coaching sessions are proactive, consistent and frequent (typically once every two weeks and last no more than 60 minutes) and are not just for a chosen few.

Professionals that engage 1-1 with prospects and clients also have the safe space to learn and practice sales skills and develop competencies. As a result, they can better respond to changing client requirements and expectations and achieve competitive success for their firms.

For further reading on building an effective internal sales coaching programme, I'd also recommend the book Coaching Salespeople into Sales Champions by Keith Rosen.

(E) – Execute

"Execution is a specific set of behaviours and techniques that companies need to master to have a competitive advantage. It's a discipline of its own."
Ram Charan and Larry Bossidy, Execution.

We've touched on the importance of strategy and culture alignment. I've highlighted some of the vital impressions that make the biggest impact on performance and results. But of course, without execution, does that all really matter?

The final and arguably most important is to develop the habit of execution. We can work on group habits and routines to get better at making impressions that matter.

But as individuals, we ultimately have a responsibility for our own success. For how we execute, that means to set our weekly and daily schedules around the small habits and routines that compound and accelerate our success over time. Take sales prospecting as an example of that. Like exercise, if we don't schedule it and make a habit of turning up (whether we like it or not), we know the consequences that can have over time.

For more on how to develop habits that stick, I've been a subscriber to the work of James Clear. His bestseller Atomic Habits and the resources that come with it are must-read.

To discover your firm's EDGE score for free, go to
https://practiceedge.scoreapp.com

Jonathan Lancaster is the Co-founder and Director of
Practice Edge **(www.practiceedge.ie)** and is a business
growth expert with a record of success with firms from
the UK and Ireland. For the past 16 years, he has helped
organisations adopt professional and ethical sales
principles to win business, increase revenue and deliver
more value to clients.

Notes

_____

_____

_____

_____

_____

_____

_____

_____

_____

_____

_____

_____

_____

_____

_____

_____

_____

_____

_____

_____

_____

_____

_____

27

Tell Stories

By Jim Irving

"Storytelling is by far the most underrated skill in business."

Gary Vaynerchuk

I have always loved books. Reading to learn something new. Reading fiction for fun and relaxation (I lean towards the thriller, detective and science fiction genres). Then helping my children to love books. Nothing in life is quite like snuggling down with a child or children at their bedtime and reading them a story – usually with voices and actions added of course!

In TV and film action series, books and theatre, frequently in (good) education what we are doing is engaging through – and immersing in - stories. Stories are how we are trained to learn and to enjoy. Throughout history, long before our digital life today, generations learned about life, their traditions, their Gods, and beliefs through stories. Handed down, time after time, they still endure today.

When we are socialising our conversation revolves around, you've guessed it, stories, and tales. Maybe current, frequently *"do you remember...?"*.

Stories are a fundamental part of every person and every society that lives, or ever lived.

And then we come to business; we base everything on facts, on slides, on collateral. We wonder why our prospects are disengaged, bored even. Knowing the above, is it any wonder?

Unlike many salespeople, I have double qualified – I am a Fellow of the professional bodies in both sales and in marketing. I have worked for many years in both. At the moment, there is a big movement in marketing towards storytelling. Why? Because of all the above. Humans are used to learning and engaging through stories, it's natural. Why construct anything else?

At a recent marketing event I heard a brand defined very differently from normal. The speaker defined the components of a brand as –

- A consistent message
- Data and proof points for that message
- Stories to explain and support the message

That was it, and do you know what, I think they were right!

Where do stories come into sales? They should be there in so many ways –

1. The reference story. "xx had the same problem, here's what happened when we engaged with them..."
2. The memory switch (aka the Columbo moment!). "Now that you mention that issue, I have just remembered..."
3. Message building. "Imagine for a moment..."
4. The fact explained. "I mentioned we do xx, well here's what that meant for Acme Co last year..."

Etc, etc etc.

And that's just in sales conversations. Where else do stories matter –

When you write a proposal do you just use a template – standard for everyone? Or do you weave in references and stories that are appropriate for them (and for their needs and priorities – assuming you have done your questioning properly)?

When you are helping to create a Whitepaper, or a blog, or an outreach email or Linkedin message is it all just facts and features? References, examples, potential usage are all more powerful than product features-based writing.

Why does this matter so much? It's simple. As humans, we are all tuned for stories. We are ready for them. Please don't fall into the features, features, features mill.

It has been the death of countless deals over the years. Let the prospect imagine their new life, understand the possibilities, and get to the point where they are telling themselves they need it.

Is this fanciful? There is an old marketing truism. As important now as ever it was. It talks to our human nature –

"We buy with our heart and then justify with our brain."

Remember the last 'thing' you wanted to buy? Did you really need it? Was it essential to you? Almost certainly not. But we fall in love with an idea, a story, a concept. We buy the 'thing'. Then we set about justifying it to ourselves – and often our spouse too!

This is as true in B2B as it is in our personal lives. Sell the story, the picture, the outcome. Become a practiced, business storyteller. Have a bank of these stories and examples ready to use – and bring them out, right when they can deliver the greatest support to your sales mission. Of course, stories need to be uplifting and positive – never negative, disparaging, or vulgar.

The lesson. Stories are central to our society, our history and to our families. Don't forget about them just because you are in a business setting. We are all human, we are all ready for that next story.

Notes

Chapter 28

Be Different, Lead with Integrity

By Larry Levine

"Integrity is choosing your thoughts and actions based on values rather than personal gain."

Chris Karcher

I believe the title of this chapter is critical to your business success. It also leaves you a better person. I will start by looking at being different and then focus in on the power of integrity. As integrity will always keep you at the top...

What sets you apart from all the other salespeople who do what you do?

Please follow along with me for a moment...

Let's say there are 15 salespeople in your marketplace who all provide similar services, solutions or products to yours; what exactly makes you different? What makes you stand out?

Why would someone do business with you?

I know what you're thinking... And quite frankly, no one cares how long you have been in your industry, how long your company has been in business, the awards they've won nor how you provide the best customer service.

Sales professionals do not hide behind their company, products, or their services. They know they are the defining factor.

Business executives are savvy. They will not engage in a business conversation or buy from you if they don't first understand why they should pay attention to you.

What sets you apart from your competition? It's up to you to prove it. I'm concerned as many in sales struggle with what sets them apart from their competition.

Think about this one... How will you grow your business in a sea full of sales sameness, where you and your competitors are viewed as interchangeable and where many buyers do not have particularly warm feelings towards you?

Sales professionals would rather be unique and stand out, as opposed to being me-too and blending in with the other empty suits.

WHY DO SO MANY IN SALES SOUND THE SAME?

We have a severe epidemic occurring within the sales world. The sales world has been bitten by the "sales sameness" bug. Unfortunately, many salespeople are telling a similar story — company centric with generic references and promises being made to help a customer's business.

Sales professionals seek to be different, not just better. Because being different makes them better.

How are you being viewed in the marketplace? I encourage you to stop hiding behind your company, your products, and your service! Stop with the generic statements, canned pitches and pretending to be interested.

Sales professionals step in front of their company and do not rely on their company for differentiation.

Sales professionals avoid swimming in the sea of sameness

WHY SHOULD SOMEONE SPEAK WITH YOU?

To be effective in opening business conversations you must speak the language of leadership. This language clearly conveys your ideas to your audience.

Use business language, not sales language, which clearly communicates to the hearts and minds of those whom you wish to move to action – your clients and ideal clients.

You must realize decision makers have more knowledge and power than ever before. They have access to information about you, your company and your competitors in ways that weren't available years ago.

Attention spans are short. You must come to the realization that you have less time with executives to create and demonstrate value, as they are arriving to the business table with a much higher bar for you to clear.

I love this quote from Ellen DeGeneres,

"I personally like being unique. I like being my own person with my own style and my own opinions and my own toothbrush."

BE DIFFERENT... BRING VISION AND VALUE

I encourage you to start engaging in conversation with executives by offering a compelling vision of the future by looking through the lens of their company and how they can prepare themselves for the future.

Bring vision cemented in a deep understanding of the trends shaping their market, their industry challenges, what their competitors may be doing and how this can help transform their company.

Rise up, accept that 'CHANGE' is necessary to succeed in your profession or drown within the sea of sameness.

Executives today expect, crave and demand, understanding and sophistication!

You must lead with intelligent insight and exciting ideas that teach them something surprising and new. And if you don't, you have now become an endangered sales species by giving them little more than what they've already read online.

What value do you bring in that situation?

Find some alone time and reflect upon these two questions...

- How can I differentiate myself with insight?
- Where can I get insight?

A sales professional knows what makes them valuable, do you?

TO DIFFERENTIATE, YOU MUST DEFINE YOURSELF

To avoid swimming in sales sameness, you must make a commitment to yourself. You must be willing to look inside yourself and ask yourself...

- What makes me different?
- What words would I use to describe myself?
- What words would others use to describe me?

Once this happens, then I would encourage you to make a commitment to yourself to becoming a learner and constantly seek out the knowledge necessary to do your job better.

Success in sales comes to those who possess the kind of knowledge that makes them a trusted and necessary resource. It's not only being a resource around the product or service in question, but also around the buyer's company, products, industry and their competitors.

Sales professionals are educators. However, you can't become an educator without being a student first.

You must develop a thirst for knowledge. You must stay up-to-date on new developments, always looking for trends and changes before they happen. Bring your knowledge to the business table and prove how you can help people do better business.

Sales professionals have deep institutional knowledge of their clients, do you?

Education differentiates the sales professionals from the sales pretenders

A sales professional doesn't overcomplicate things. They equip themselves with the right combination of data and human insight to become a problem-solver.

SWIM IN A DIFFERENT OCEAN

It's sad and concerning that so many in sales fall into the me-too category. They hang out with other me-too reps. They swim in mediocrity. They complain about the same things.

They all hold hands and sing Kumbaya while drowning within the sea of sameness.

What would a business executive uncover if they decided to do some research on you?

Business executives are sleuths.

- How are you publicly demonstrating your expertise?
- Are you actively engaged in business conversations?
- Are you demonstrating leadership in your market?

Why on earth would someone devote time to speak with you? Where does this leave you?

Louis D. Brandeis said it best,
"In differentiation, not in uniformity, lies the path of progress."

Are you focused on truly differentiating yourself? What about your standards?

"Real integrity is doing the right thing, knowing that nobody's going to know whether you did it or not."
Oprah Winfrey

In a post-trust sales world, you must bring integrity forward every single day. You must live it, breathe it, and demonstrate it. Living with integrity especially in sales takes courage.

Let's look at **INTEGRITY** through the lens of Wikipedia...

"Integrity is the practice of being honest and showing a consistent and uncompromising adherence to strong moral and ethical principles and values."

Two questions for all those in sales, sales management, and leadership...

- How many of your clients and future clients would define salespeople as being honest?
- Would your clients and future clients use the words moral and ethical in your approach to working with them?

WHY INTEGRITY IN SALES IS IMPORTANT

What are your sales morals? Living your sales life full of integrity is the only way, especially in a world where trust is almost non-existent. The way you conduct yourself reflects upon your character and builds your reputation.

A life of integrity means you never have to spend time or energy questioning yourself. When you listen to your heart and do the right thing, your sales life becomes simple. And, by the way, this applies equally in your personal life too.

Your actions and the way you conduct yourself are open for your clients and future clients to see.

Acting with integrity gives you peace of mind in knowing you did the right thing regardless of the outcome.

You are responsible for your own conduct, and you are responsible for your own integrity. Living with integrity is daunting. How many in sales are drawn to the 'dark side' where ego, fear, and commission breath run our every thought? Let's face it, this happens to all of us. Therefore, we must regularly make adjustments and about-face U-turns to bring integrity back into the forefront of our lives.

Are your words and actions in alignment with your beliefs and values?

"The reputation of a thousand years may be determined by the conduct of one hour."
Japanese Proverb

Are you guarding your reputation?

INTEGRITY, A KEY COMPONENT OF SELLING FROM THE HEART

No longer does old-school bravado and a bragging mindset work in today's sales climate. No one gives a rip what you've accomplished in your sales career. They want to know how much you care about them. This is where I strongly believe servant-led leadership comes in, learning how to serve with heartfelt sincerity and integrity.

The word "integrity" comes from the Latin "integritas," meaning wholeness and soundness.

Are you serving your clients with wholeness and soundness?

"The servant-leader is servant first... It begins with the natural feeling that one wants to serve, to serve first."
Robert K. Greenleaf

Learning how to serve, leading your life with integrity, and selling from the heart; mix these together and this becomes a recipe for a very fulfilling sales career. Salespeople who have a strong sense of integrity are sadly a rare breed in today's business world.

HERE ARE A FEW TRAITS ASSOCIATED WITH INTEGRITY FILLED PROFESSIONALS -

"Integrity gives you real freedom because you have nothing to fear since you have nothing to hide."
Zig Ziglar

Integrity, said author C.S. Lewis, "is doing the right thing, even when no one is looking." Integrity is a foundational moral virtue. This must be brought back into the sales profession. I am curious to know... What does your moral courage look like? In fact, how would you define moral courage?

Acting with integrity in sales means accepting that you will always conduct yourself in accordance with honesty, fairness, and plain decency.

Salespeople with integrity share some of these traits...

- They are always honest
- They never take advantage of their clients
- They are humble
- They give without expecting anything in return
- They never manipulate their clients
- They see the good in their clients

In a world full of empty suits, integrity will keep you at the top.

Are you leading your sales life with integrity? What can you do practically to audit yourself? You can make an accurate assessment by asking yourself these questions devised by ThinkHR, a human resource compliance company.

- Am I willing to say what I'm thinking?
- Am I willing to risk being wrong?
- Does this conduct make me a better person?
- Am I leading by example?
- Am I taking 100% responsibility?

Never ever waiver from your integrity. After all, we expect it from others, don't we!

Integrity is essential in relational contentment and fulfilment.

A poem by Frank Outlaw

"Watch your thoughts; They become your words.

Watch your words; They become your actions.

Watch your actions; They become your habits.

Watch your habits; They become your character.

Watch your character; It becomes your destiny."

Are you doing the right thing only because it is the right thing for your clients? Or are you doing it for yourself first, as well as others?

Integrity in sales is doing the right things right even if it costs you.

Larry Levine is the best-selling author of Selling from the Heart and the co-host of the Selling from the Heart Podcast. In a post trust sales world, Larry Levine helps sales teams leverage the power of authenticity to grow revenue, grow themselves and enhance the lives of their clients.

Larry has coached sales professionals across the world, from tenured reps to new millennials entering the salesforce. They all appreciate the practical, real, raw, relevant, relatable and "street-savvy" nature of his coaching. Larry is not shy when it comes to delivering his message.

Larry is leading a revolution and a movement of authenticity, integrity, and substance in the sales profession.

Larry believes people would rather do business with a sales professional who sells from the heart as opposed to a sales rep who is an empty suit.

You can reach Larry Levine at:
llevine@sellingfromtheheart.net

You can learn about the movement being created with Selling for the Heart at **www.sellingfromtheheart.net**

Lastly, you can follow Larry Levine on LinkedIn at
https://www.linkedin.com/in/larrylevine1992/

Notes

Chapter

29

The Psychology of Selling

By Jamie Martin

"Psychology is probably the most important factor in the market – and one that is least understood."

David Dreman

Selling is all about people. Considering that fact, it is critical that we do all we can to understand human behaviour, communication and how best to build rapport. Doing so can have a massive impact on your sales and business career. This chapter gives just a very short insight into some basic, introductory thinking in these areas. It also provides some really useful tips to help you improve your memory...

Some Psychological Behaviours

The average Human attention span within a learning situation e.g., a lecture, is approximately 8 seconds *(Bradbury, 2016)*. Why is this an important starting point for my chapter? It's simple – this of course means that your first impressions really count!

This fact should impact your approach to your sales copy/email/social media content. All these need to be tightly aligned and focussed on your target audience, as well as attention grabbing, and memorable!

But, as important, the principle also applies in our verbal communications. What we say – and how we say it – is critical as we engage with our prospects. What will have impact, interest and intrigue them? And here's a clue, it's definitely not a rushed, blurted product pitch! Their interest will only peak if we offer them potential value and proof of our capabilities.

Early research, since confirmed, by *Dale Edgar* tells us that when we are learning new information, we retain **10%** (when reading), **20%** (when hearing), **30%** (when seeing), and **90%** (when doing). Now, the actual percentages don't really matter. But the underlying principle really does. For example, knowing this, how could you improve your prospects retention of information during a presentation/ demo meeting? What practical steps can you take to increase their engagement, enjoyment and likelihood of agreeing with you? Listening isn't going to do it for them...

Next, we move on to thinking about your prospects preferred communications style. This is another important factor in building the relationship. Serious research has gone into the how and why of individual communication. Again, some simple lessons can be taken from that research. For example, communication was found in one study to be **93%** non-verbal and **7%** verbal (*Dr. Mehrabian, 1960*). What was 'non-verbal'? He found that your body language (**55%**), the tone and pitch of your voice (**38%**), and what you say (**7%**) during communicating with your prospect will directly impact their buying experience. Once more, the actual numbers can be discussed but the general thrust is well established. If you take time to consider this, it leads you to think very carefully about how you approach prospect and customer meetings.

How does your prospect respond during a pitch meeting? Do they show signs of uncertainty by not actively listening to you? Is their body language 'uncomfortable'? Have you studied body language to help you better understand what signals are sent?

So, we have established that people either learn by or process information from visual (written information) auditory (hearing), kinaesthetic (touch), or verbal (the language context and meaning).

How would your prospect prefer to communicate with you? (Email, LinkedIn PM, WhatsApp, phone, video conference, etc). These things are individual, but you can build a persona as you do your outreach work. Is the target in a creative or process-based role? Do their conversations with you revolve around visualisation (*"I see that", "I get the picture"*) – if so, you need to make your presentation highly visual. These are just a couple of examples but tailoring your language and approach to them can deliver big results.

With any communication style/content, always personalise it to your specific target prospect to improve their attention and memory. Apply the concept by *Frank Hutchinson Dukesmith* (**AIDA:** Attention, Interest, Desire, Action).

Advice: Just ask your B2B prospect for their preferred correspondence style, as well as the best days and times to contact them. Adapt your approach based on this detail to improve the prospect's buying experience.

Psychological Business Rapport

Building a strong synergy and rapport with your prospect earlier on within the buying experience improves conversion.

It would be ideal if you and your prospect knew something about each other personally, shared a similar interest and hobby, or you both had a similar experience in a previous business life. Finding out this key information will provide you with insights about your prospect's personality, character, and how they prefer to do business.

"When people are like each other they tend to like each other."
Tony Robbins

When the prospect raises objections or negotiations occur during the buying experience, you are already armed with what and how to respond to your prospect to maintain their interest in working with you, especially if they already 'like' you from the rapport building stage.

*Bob Burg quotes the renowned **KLT** phrase (Know, Like, Trust).*

Prospects who trust you are more likely to work with you/ buy from you. Research suggests when people are decision making, they make judgments **90%** based on emotion and **10%** based on logical thinking.

During your presentation/demonstration (particularly at the needs-based selling stage), mention case studies or experiences that resonate with the prospect's emotions (from feeling happy to fear of missing out). The prospect will remember the times when they have also experienced these emotions and are more likely to proceed to then buy for a desired outcome or to avoid a negative situation.

For some of the above guidance, this would be once you have engaged with the prospect. What about if you are starting cold with a prospect? How can you identify useful details about your prospect to mention in your first interactions prior to approaching them?

Advice: research your competitors! Find out from their clients what they liked/did not like about their service/product & adapt your approach based on these clients' feedback. How else could you stand out from your competition – what are they doing/not doing? (Sign up to their newsletters, etc. to find out).

Improving Your Memory

Learning and remembering new information can be challenging, particularly in the stress of a meeting or call. Here are some techniques to improve your memory:

Think about when you want to memorise or learn a new pitch. During a new information learning experience, your attention span and memory will only sustain for a short period of time. So, be selective and focus your time spent on learning and rehearsing the most important content – that which will, most likely, help to increase your sales. Here are a couple more 'tricks' to aid memory retention. Having 'good' smells present or eating memory boosting foods (for example dark chocolate) are also useful in linking learning content and subsequent memory retention. This can be useful when you control the environment when you are learning or developing new techniques within sales.

Use acronyms to remember key benefits or features of your service/product. From a psychological perspective, a study by *Purves et al, 2008;* identifies the short-term working memory being able to support more words when the words are short compared to long words. This sounds obvious, doesn't it, but how often do we use big words and phrases when shorter and simpler will do? Apply acronyms or abbreviations to help you remember your sales pitch details. 'Go simple' in your language. When presenting visually or in a written proposal to a prospect, this linguistic process of 'shortening' words and content will help with remembering the most important elements. And it works both ways. They will learn more and retain it better when you focus on using simpler language.

When writing content down, apply the 'chunking' process (selecting smaller parts – just the core message – from the larger body of information). The chunked elements will be easier to remember for both the salesperson and prospect during a sales pitch. Rehearsing these chunked notes will trigger your memory to remember more from that larger piece of information, ready to deliver this content in a B2B sales context.

Visual content (images/videos/products) has a strong impact on memory, especially when this material resonates with emotional thinking. Creating personalised visual content for your prospects during their buying journey will improve sales conversion. This action will demonstrate your passion to work with this prospect, make you stand out from your competition during the presentation/ demonstration stage, and the prospect will remember this visual information more strongly for their subsequent decision-making process.

Now here's a simple fact! Regularly reading sales books or listening to sales podcasts will increase your knowledge of this topic. Being exposed and revisiting similar content often will continually improve your memory of this content, ready to outperform the competition with specific details and techniques when selling to your prospects.

Create supporting stories ready for your B2B pitches (stories are effective for your memory processing i.e., remembering statistics/figures). Research suggests storytelling during sales pitches can improve their retention of information. Speak words/pitches aloud (to identify any errors in your content, inflection or presentation). Practice everything until perfect!

This is just a very brief introduction to a very big world, full of ways to improve your performance and success. I hope you found it useful.

Jamie Martin BSc (Hons), PGCert is Managing Director & Founder of Correct Careers Coaching (modern sales training and sales strategy business).

Jamie is an award-winning modern Sales Coach and Trainer, cocreator of a B2B sales e-Learning course, as well as an author, podcaster, and speaker.

Jamie is passionate about sales strategy, social media, and sales training to help businesses improve their revenue and processes.

Correct Careers Coaching delivers modern sales training (full sales cycle) including social media marketing/prospecting, lead generation, new business conversion, client relationship management, negotiation, as well as Jamie's own pioneering programme 'Sales Psychology'.

Jamie Martin
T: +44 (0)7599 332178
E: Jamie@correctcareerscoaching.com
https://correctcareerscoaching.com
https://www.linkedin.com/in/jamiemartin111

Notes

Chapter

30

Working Successfully with Partners

By Vince Menzione

"If everyone is moving forward together, then success takes care of itself."

Henry Ford

Why should you have a focus on a partner-driven model? It's a question I have been asked many times. Working with partners and developing a successful partnership isn't easy. But done properly, it can deliver enormous value to any business. The benefits are numerous; a bigger presence, more 'feet on the street', broader geographic coverage, an easier path into new vertical sectors and the ability to punch above your weight. In addition, proactive partners can help you spot new market opportunities and move faster towards opportunity. This applies equally if you are a large corporate/manufacturer or a small business aiming to create a bigger presence by partnering with bigger players.

My working life has been spent in the Tech industry. It's fair to say that the tech industry is driven by partnerships. From innovation to reselling, companies big and small collaborate to bring transformation to customers. Heightened uncertainty and the pace of digital transformation has increased pressure on partners to move swiftly as industry demands evolve, with smart partnerships emerging as a crucial strategy. Yet there continues to be a lack of consensus, or even understanding, around what qualities an organization needs to build successful partnerships. This has been my focus for over 25 years, beginning as a general manager of partner strategy at Microsoft, and eventually as the alliance lead at a billion-dollar partner. Through my experience leading organizations, coaching, and interviewing influential leaders on my podcast, I've now identified several core pillars of success for partnering in the technology sector. I also believe – and multiple conversations have confirmed – that these core pillars also apply to any business seeking to work with partners.

My podcast 'Ultimate Guide to Partnering' is a laboratory for exploring the science of high-performance partnerships. We've come a long way since the podcast launched in 2016 with the simple goal of helping some 350,000 Microsoft partners position themselves for the tech transformation ahead. Over the course of the first 60 episodes (now at 120 episodes and counting...), my guests and I unpacked not only the principles of a successful partner, but the personal and professional journey – the grit, determination, and resolve - that drives a person to overcome obstacles to do and be more.

After a brief hiatus when I pursued a "dream job" with a billion-dollar Microsoft partner, I revived the podcast in June 2020 with a renewed conviction that partnership can accelerate growth and sustain survival during challenging seasons. Experience from both sides – as a Microsoft channel chief and also as a partner to a tech giant – rounded out my understanding of what was required to make partnership successful for both parties, and I was eager to share it with partners searching for a lifeboat.

Digital transformation is rapidly changing the role of partnerships

We've all experienced a rapid transformation to our economy, culture, and lifestyle over the past year. The role of technology has been unmistakable as nearly everyone was forced to pivot to a world of virtual work and school, shopping and socializing. Satya Nadella, Microsoft's CEO, captured the intensity of the moment when he noted that *"we've seen two years' worth of digital transformation in two months."*

There will be no "return to normal." As Jay McBain, a prominent analyst at Forrester, recently said on my podcast. He indicated that 76% of CEO's today – in every industry in every geography – believe that their current business model will be unrecognizable in five years.

Lightweight, point solutions are displacing monolithic systems alongside the growing consumerization of commercial IT. We see glimpses of this in companies like IBM, Dell, HP, and Cisco who are jettisoning their services business or committing to 100% consumption business models. Consequently, the partnership channel is also transforming. Influencer strategies are replacing resale and distribution and marketplaces are becoming more prevalent. As Martin Casado, General Manager of VC form Andreessen Horowitz, recently wrote, *"cloud marketplaces aren't just one channel for selling software – it's becoming THE channel."*

So, if partnering is so common and so essential, why do organizations still struggle here? Generally speaking, the answer is *culture*. Whether risk-aversion, arrogance, or a stubborn allegiance to an old business model, disordered organizational cultures can stifle the growth of a healthy partner program. Alternately, organizations that recognize the importance of partnering to their financial growth and commit to developing a growth mindset will improve their ability to ride the waves of change in an economy rife with uncertainty.

Adopting the following attributes can help organizations big and small, across diverse sectors and regions, achieve greater agility now and into the future.

1. Growth mindset
Building and cultivating a partner channel requires you to be open-minded, growth-oriented, and vulnerable. Organizations with a growth mindset reward risk-taking and a "fail-fast" approach to change. I call this Business Darwinism. But change is not easy. Building successful partnerships often requires embracing a different approach. During this time of uncertainty, realizing that partners can add value and amplify the message with an "abundance" frame of reference can yield positive results.

2. Shared vision
Stakeholder groups must agree to a shared vision and a compelling value proposition with objectives, result areas, metrics and milestones for attainment. Big, bold,

and innovative, the vision and plan to achieve it must involve and inspire all stakeholders. Clarifying this vision will inform better decisions about people, strategies, processes, finances, and customers. Clear expectations form the foundation of enduring partnerships.

3. Extreme commitment

From my work in and around the Microsoft partner ecosystem, I have found that organizations that "got it right" were committed to changing the business model at the top – having the right people in the right seats with an agreed-upon level of commitment toward partnership execution. In other words, alignment. For change management to be successful, every department in the company needs to buy in.

4. Consistent communication

Once your vision is on paper, ensure that every member of the organization hears it clearly and consistently. When everyone's energy is going in the same direction, their accumulated drive will kick in and create an exponential force.

5. Maniacal focus

Rather than boiling the ocean, successful partnerships often require stripping out complexity and friction to focus on the "one thing" that the two organizations can accomplish together. When both partners are aligned around a single goal, you'll be quicker to find synergies and overcome challenges for greater results. Remember, a few watts of energy concentrated in one direction is all a laser beam needs to cut through diamonds.

6. Brand elevation

As a group, tech organizations have been slow to embrace the power of brand across their audience groups. However, brand and brand storytelling have emerged as critical elements to partnering success. What your brand is known for and how well you tell your story has a real influence on how internal stakeholders, customers, and partners approach their relationship with you. Only when the culture you build around growth-mindset and shared vision is reflected in your public-facing brand and amplified by brand storytelling, can it fulfil its potential as a catalyst for growth.

7. Results-orientation

Successful partnerships are built around a clearly defined process and set of mutually agreed-upon metrics designed to maximize results. Applying a co-sell methodology and operating model aligns sales processes and procedures and creates visibility. It also enables results to be tracked, shared, and evaluated through cadence and attribution. They drive the right level of traction to deliver results which, at the end of the day, is where the rubber meets the road.

8. Agility

Achieving dexterity in business is critical in the current environment. One way to build this into your business is to explore new business opportunities through micro-investments and partnerships. A partner once told me on the podcast that *"you have to be able to invest in a controlled fashion in areas that you think or ... know are tremendous opportunities that may be too early for anyone to have recognized."* A practice of strategic partnership allows organizations to nimbly test markets and business approaches and maintain the ability to pivot.

If done well, partnering can be a force multiplier for reaching a new market or adding new solutions and capabilities that drive successful outcomes. Leaders who integrate these principles into their company practices will not only see their existing partnerships flourish but will put themselves in a better position to accelerate their channel strategy as digital transformation continues to evolve every aspect of our lives.

In my world, over 20 years ago, the then CEO of HP was asked *"Why are you being so successful with your channel business?".* His answer was surprising to some, but truly showed a core partnering attitude. *"We have only one salesforce. True, it's split into two groups – 'on salary' and 'off salary', but it's a single salesforce. That's what has delivered our success".* Do you really have a single salesforce or is it still a bit 'us and them'?

As I reflect on the journey that brought me to the 100th episode of my podcast, I'm reminded of a quote from the remarkable Nazi concentration camp survivor, Dr Viktor Frankl, in his book, *Man's Search for Meaning: "The last of one's freedoms is to choose one's attitude..."*
If we have seen anything over the past year, it is that transformation is coming whether we like it or not. I firmly believe that holding an attitude that embraces change will lead to more successful outcomes for our business partnerships and a more positive impact on our world and society.

Vince Menzione is the host of The Ultimate Guide to Partnering podcast and Ultimate Partnerships, an IT consulting firm focused on helping organizations reach their goals with successful partnering. With nearly a decade of experience as manager of partner strategy with Microsoft and tenures at partner companies, Vince's wrap-around knowledge of partnership has uniquely equipped him to help organizations navigate partnerships for mutual and sustainable success.

E: vincem@ultimate-partnerships.com
www.linkedin.com/in/vincemenzione

Notes

_____

_____

_____

_____

_____

_____

_____

_____

_____

_____

_____

_____

_____

_____

_____

_____

_____

_____

_____

_____

_____

_____

_____

_____

_____

31

Top 10 Pricing Tips in B2B Sales

By Mark Peacock

*"Price is what you pay.
Value is what you get."*

Warren Buffett

In the B2B sales environment, it's very common to see salespeople using price as a tactic for closing a sale by offering discounts or price reductions.

Whilst this may sometimes be necessary, in my experience it is more often a result of a poorly thought-out pricing strategy and a lack of discipline regarding price in the sales team.

If you turn the question on its head and ask yourself *"how can we charge more for what we do?"*, you might be surprised at some of the things you can uncover.

There are plenty of simple, yet relatively unknown pricing tactics that can make a huge difference to your sales performance. Many of them take inspiration from behavioural economics and from an understanding of the psychology of pricing. Businesses who fail to learn about these simple techniques will often be leaving money on the table.

And if you are working in a B2B sales environment, you should ideally be focussed on profit targets rather than revenue targets. This will change the focus of the sales team from chasing volume (at the expense of profit), to chasing a better balance between volume and price (to achieve more profitability).

Here are my top 10 tips on pricing tactics that any business could use to improve pricing and profit margins.

1. Create a **high price anchor** for a premium option and mention this before you mention your standard price. *"Our premium product/service is £1,000 or alternatively you can take our regular product/service for £500."* The regular price now looks very attractive when compared to the premium price.

2. Use the **power of 3** when it comes to your prices, with a high price, a mid-price and a low price for each customer (e.g., £1,000, £500 or £300). This will increase the chances of you closing the sale and achieving higher revenue as well.

3. Sell your prices from **high to low**, not low to high. Always mention your highest price first and then, as needed, reveal your lower prices. This is far more powerful than saying "prices from..." (which all sales and marketing people the world over have a tendency to say at the start of any conversation)

4. Incentivise your sales teams on **gross profit** rather than just revenue or volume. They will be forced to achieve a better balance between price and volume, rather than just going for more volume and revenue (at the expense of profit).

5. Train your sales teams on how to **sell value, rather than price**. Most salespeople are too quick to lower prices when dealing with objections, as they haven't been properly trained on how to sell value. *"I know the investment is £30,000, but we have already agreed that the first-year payback alone will be over £100,000."*

6. Ask prospects or lost customers for **feedback on your prices.** *"How important was price in your decision to use/not use our services?"* You might be surprised to find that it is less often about price and is more often about other aspects of your proposition that didn't quite meet the buyer's requirements.

7. **Halve all your discounts.** If you have a standard range of volume discounts, e.g., between 10% – 40%, halve all your discounts to 5% to 20% (without changing your prices). You will be amazed at how simple and effective this change can be, and it will provide an immediate boost to your profits without any noticeable damage to your sales rates.

8. **Calculate the impact of a 1% increase** in your prices, and what difference this will make to your net profits. A good rule of thumb is that a 1% increase in price yields a 10% increase in net profits. This analysis can be very worthwhile to your business.

9. When implementing **price increases**, follow industry norms when it comes to the timing. If everyone else increases their prices in January, you should do the same. Put a plan together at least 3 months in advance and clearly explain why your prices are going up. It's OK to use cost increases as part of the reason, but you still have to sell hard on the benefits of why the customer should continue using your products or services. Treat a price increase campaign as you would a sales opportunity for a new prospect, and don't take your existing customers for granted.

10. Finally, **think ahead to your next financial year** and aim to set higher price points for your products. Then work out a plan for how you can achieve that higher price position (e.g., by adding more value or features to your products or by having better trained salespeople). Your primary goal should be to increase your average selling price over time, rather than just achieve revenue growth. Price improvement will drive much higher profit growth than revenue growth.

Don't be afraid to embrace the world of pricing. Too many salespeople see it as a scary subject and will train themselves on how to deal with price objections. But as the customer representative in your organisation, you should know best what value your company's products and services deliver to your customers.

So, learn how to price more creatively and, using some of the techniques outlined above, find new ways to price what you do rather than using the same old pricing model everyone in your industry has used for years.

Always remember, a small increase in a price can make a massive difference to your net profits. Anybody can sell by dropping to a cheaper price, but it takes a bit of effort and creative thinking to sell value at higher prices. And business owners will be far more appreciative of salespeople who can sell more profitable contracts than those who win sales leagues for selling the most volume!

Mark Peacock, Managing Director, PriceMaker Ltd
Mark Peacock is one of the UK's leading experts on pricing and a specialist in helping businesses improve their pricing strategy. Pricing is fundamental to every business, yet most people don't spend enough time thinking about it. Mark's mission is to educate businesses so that they can learn how to optimise their price positioning, increase their prices with integrity and sell their prices with confidence. Mark is the founder of PriceMaker Ltd, a specialist pricing consultancy based in London that works with a wide range of businesses in the B2B sector – tech, services, manufacturing, and marketing. Visit **www.pricemaker.co.uk** for a free assessment of your pricing capability.

Notes

_____

_____

_____

_____

_____

_____

_____

_____

_____

_____

_____

_____

_____

_____

_____

_____

_____

_____

_____

_____

_____

_____

32 | The Three Reasons Model

By Jim Irving

"The most important thing we learn at school is that the most important things aren't learned at school."

Haruki Marukami

In life, in business, and in selling there are some core truths. Some of these are widely known, others are much less commonly understood. But because they are core truths each is very important. Here are some examples –

"Don't sell before you understand your customer – questions first"

"Look both ways before you cross the road"

"Qualify continuously"

"Don't eat yellow snow"

All these types of truths just... exist. They were true yesterday, are just as true today and will be true in the future – they are, in effect, constants. We ignore them at our peril...

This chapter is all about another truth – the 'Three Reasons Model'.

When you are selling, one of the big questions you need to ask is *"why are they buying?"*.

As you engage with the DMU (all of those with a voice in the potential purchase decision – the customer's Decision Making Unit) you should be thinking about their individual perspectives and language.

Put simply; if the person is from finance, they will usually view the world through the lens of numbers, HR through people, operations through process, IT through systems and software etc. Great professional salespeople take this into account and adjust their phrasing and approach depending on who they are speaking to at the time. Each specialist inside your prospect will NOT expect you to be an expert in their domain, but they will really appreciate if you try to communicate with them in their terms. As people, they will like you more for doing that.

But what drives an organisation to spend money in the first place?

We immediately think of things like efficiency, competitive advantage, replacing old equipment or software, improving customer service. I would suggest that these are some of the basic drivers. But what are the underlying outcomes they are seeking. Imagine the CEO, sitting at the top, agreeing or refusing spend requests, pulling the organisational strings. What are their drivers? At the highest level what do organisations choose to spend money on? What are they trying to achieve?

If you are brave or have a strong opinion, try to think like your biggest prospect – right now. Cover the rest of this chapter up and try to specify yourself, what their high-level drivers are. I will leave you some space to do exactly that...

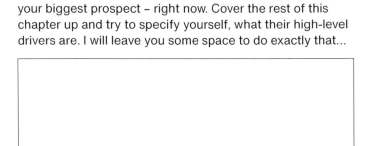

Many years ago, I was training a group of highly professional salespeople in the City of London. We were half-way through the sessions when a guest speaker arrived. During their talk they covered this exact subject. They were in a very senior position in a major bank. Controlling expenditure. They knew about this specific topic – they lived it.

The individual asked for ideas on what these reasons might be. Lots of hands went up, the sort of answers I suggested above, were thrown at him. After a while he smiled, said they were all quite good answers, but that they were missing the overall perspective. He then explained the reality. All my ideas above, and those shouted at him were part of the story, but they weren't the underlying reason or justification. In each case they were just steps towards an overall corporate objective.

What are the real, core, underlying reasons for money being allocated to projects – or not? The 'Three Reasons Model' cuts away everything else and brings you to those central, core drivers. Here they are –

Organisations spend money for only three reasons –

1. To **improve profits or revenues** (depending on their focus, either growth or profitability).
2. To **reduce their costs** (the efficiency story)
3. To **reduce their risks** (these can be around new legislation, competitive risk, legal and contractual risks)

Everything else falls into one or more of these categories. Simple, isn't it?

Some thoughts on those three reasons –

- It is obvious that any commercial organisation has an ultimate growth/profit/revenue goal. That's so easy to see. But you might say, what about those non-profit organisations? Trusts? Government bodies, public health, and charities for example. They don't have that goal. And you would be right. But they do have an equivalent. Every single one has priorities and an ultimate goal. Say you are a UK hospital, for example. Each year the regional or national governing body sets their targets – *"reduce the xx waiting list", "improve operational outcomes in a specific area"* and others. These become their 'public sector' version of that ultimate driver. Here's a question for you. Do you know the revenue and/or profit targets your commercial prospects have set for the year? Do you know the operational goals mandated from above for your public sector customers? If you don't, how can you show where you can help them?

- Risk reduction is usually the one that most individuals find hardest to get first time. Profit and costs are easy, but what about risk? ALL organisations will happily spend money to reduce their risks. These could be legislative – laws they must adhere too, especially new ones coming down the line or perhaps compliance – ensuring the business is doing what is required by their governing body/profession/authorities. Personal risk also comes into play here. How much will a Board pay to ensure they are protected (in any way they can be) from things like corporate manslaughter charges, individual culpability, customer lawsuits? This spend has nothing to do with revenues or costs, but everything to do with reducing their corporate and personal risk.

- I have had salespeople say, *"but how do I get to a specific message on these?"*. The answer is simpler than you might think and it's just three letters – WMT. **Which Means That.** Using those three simple words, or the vast number of alternatives you can use, leads you directly to those three outcomes. *"Using this technology will help you get to market 3 months earlier...**which means that** your revenues will rise by £1m a month, much quicker than planned. That will directly improve your annual revenues this year by £3m".* Or *"By using this compliance software, you will be aligned to the governments new standards. **This will lead you** to avoid potential corporate fines of up to £5m AND ensure your personal compliance too".* WMT is an enormously powerful tool that all salespeople can use. It takes you from a soft, woolly, message to something that directly impacts your prospect.

Now of course, reducing costs can also help to improve profits. These three items are connected but very distinct approaches/priorities.

What does this have to do with sales? Well, if you are selling and are fixated on your features, how do they – exactly – deliver against these three goals? I bet they don't.

If you talk in general terms and hit none of the three reasons, are you going to be prioritised for spend? Of course not. When analysed, your proposal will fall way short of helping them achieve their core objectives. And it will very likely be rejected.

So, when making first contact, discussing your solution, presenting, demonstrating, and then creating your proposal, always keep those three fundamental drivers at the front of your thinking. Show what you can do to help them achieve one, two or even three of these goals and you will be far closer to a win.

Oh, and by the way, I have sat in that very seat at the head of a large organisation. Even the biggest companies have budget constraints and limited spend, so they prioritise where their precious money goes. The finance department will use tools like IRR (Internal Rate of return), RoI (Return on Investment) and even ROCE (Return on Capital Employed) to help them make these decisions. If your proposal isn't specific on the likely outcomes and another is, guess which will win...

Finally, never ever forget, that when you are trying to gain some unplanned spend, your competition isn't just other competitive vendors in your own specialist area, it's anywhere that money could be allocated. Make sure your proposal is specific and compelling when it comes to the 'Three Reasons' and the outcomes they will achieve. I once lost a world-wide software and hardware solution to a fleet of trucks!

The lesson. Think like your customer. Ask them what their priorities are. Focus on delivering specific outcomes for them. Focus on their 'Three Reasons'. Therein lies the path to success.

Notes

_____

_____

_____

_____

_____

_____

_____

_____

_____

_____

_____

_____

_____

_____

_____

_____

_____

_____

_____

_____

_____

_____

_____

Chapter

33 | Listen to Your Customer!

By Tracey Roberts

"If you don't listen to your customers, someone else will."

Sam Walton

I lived in the world of corporate IT during a long and successful career. I then dabbled in the world of the tech start-up before I finally decided to go and do what I should have done much earlier!

I am now the proud founder and owner of Dive Rutland, a small but fast growing and highly successful diving business. We have been running for six years+ now. I have managed to achieve the highest ratings and qualifications in the diving world, so I now train everyone from absolute beginners to diving instructors and am a service technician for various manufacturers diving equipment.

The business operates across a few areas but is focussed on our training and retail centre. It's here that I have learned a fair bit about the world of sales – from both sides...

First in B2C selling, to as broad a range of customers as you could ever find, each with their own needs and preferences. Our customers come in all shapes and sizes and bring their knowledge, or lack of knowledge, and ideas with them to every engagement. A lot of what we sell is expensive and complex, so this is typically a full-service sale. We are experts but our customers always have their own opinions.

What's my biggest single piece of learning? That is so easy. Please just listen to your customer. When we started out, we found ourselves learning everything about every product and then regurgitating it all to every person who then visited us. Guess what, sales were OK, but not great.

Then we realised, if the person walked in and said, *"I like the look of that pink one",* you must talk to them about colours and colour options, not the technical aspects of the 2-stage diving regulator. I know this may sound simple but visiting other diving centres I have experienced this issue as a customer. And in car dealerships. I am sure you have too. There seems to be a compulsion to tell everyone everything, without taking a breath and listening. It seems to me that this is one of the most common mistakes salespeople make. They are scripted and just waiting for the opportunity to start pitching. That doesn't build a relationship or make the other person comfortable.

In fact, sometimes the salesperson does not even speak directly to the purchaser! Take the example of my husband and I in a car showroom, the salesperson kept talking to my husband about the car, even though he was told on several times that the car was for me – the only question I got asked was what colour interior I wanted! Guess what, I walked out, and they lost the sale.

We now focus on asking questions, really listening to the answers and only then talking to them about their needs in their language and style. This works so much better and makes our visitors much more relaxed and comfortable with us. They spend more too. Why, because they trust us because we listen!

And in some circumstances having the courage to walk away from the sale because the customer is only interested in getting the cheapest price was a very hard lesson to learn – have confidence in your product and your value!

Second, I am, of course, now regularly sold to by B2B salespeople. Wow. What an education that has been. Some are superb – informed, interested, keen to help us in our business, asking questions and exploring the options. In the early days this was not common, in fact, the majority were very poor!! We were hit with pre-prepared pitches, aggression, and flaky tactics all the time.

Not so much now, as some have learnt the hard way with us, this is not the way to work or handle us. Those who have learned and who listen, question, and work in partnership are doing very well with us.

To be clear, we are growing fast, the equipment we stock can be VERY expensive, we get lots of repeat business from our customers. So, you would think that we are a prime target from those who want to sell their products through us. It doesn't always seem that way.

1. Why don't salespeople research? They call or visit with no idea of who we are, what we specialise in doing, what our customers say about us. They appear, deliver a pitch and hope some of it sticks. Well, it pretty always doesn't.
2. That lack of preparation can lead to some seriously missed opportunities. Let me give you an example which is both funny and oh so sad at the same time. If you visit our website **(www.diverutland.com)** it only takes three clicks, let me say that again, three clicks, to get to 'meet the team'. There I am right up front; 'Tracey – The Boss'. Yet every month we have (outside Covid) multiple visits from male salespeople who will walk in and talk to the male staff member who works for me. How do you think those conversations go? Three clicks...

So, whether you are buying or selling, B2B or B2C, listen to your customer. REALLY listen. And before you even meet them, at least find out the basics. Turning up just isn't good enough today.

Tracey Roberts is the owner and founder of Dive Rutland Limited, but prior to that she managed IT support teams for various organisations including Barclays Wealth Management. She has always concentrated on team relationships and providing high quality, customer focused service and that continues to this very day. Patience is her middle name! She likes to mentor individuals, working with their strengths and weaknesses with the aim to always make them the best they can be by utilising their individual learning styles.

Notes

Chapter

34

Thinking Like a Buyer

By Mark Schenkius

"Empathy is the ultimate form of customer insight."

Don Peppers

'A buyers hell'

Today is the day. After months of preparation, I am truly excited to see what today brings. I have been heavily involved in running an RFP process for logistics services over the last few months and for today we have selected four suppliers to come and present their proposal to both the logistics manager and myself as the buyer. Together we'll decide which two suppliers will go through to the final stage of the process.

Some suppliers I haven't even met face-to-face since it has mainly been a desktop exercise until now. We have planned four sessions of two hours each so it's going to be a full day today.

The first supplier arrives late. *"Apologies, sincere apologies for being late. We were stuck in traffic. There has been an accident..."* All I hear is *"bla bla bla".* I refrain myself from saying: *"If you can't manage your own logistics, how can you manage ours".* Instead, I decide to give them the benefit of the doubt.

Next, they introduce themselves as the owner of the company and the operations manager. We introduce ourselves as well. In the meantime, their operations manager tries to connect their laptop to the beamer. It doesn't seem to work. He says that normally he never has any issues with this, but I can hear him thinking: *"hopefully it will work out this time since I have been having troubles with my laptop for a few weeks now. I should have got this issue checked".* We can't seem to get it to work, so he decides to put the presentation on a USB-stick, and I run the presentation for him on my laptop. Finally, we're ready to go.

Roughly, the first 30 of 76 slides are all about the company's history, dating back to 1958 when his grandfather bought his first truck and grandmother was looking after administrative tasks. Since then, they have grown organically and through acquisitions... I struggle to focus and as I am watching the screen, I am thinking to myself: 56 slides left, 55, 54... When does the hurting end?

Finally, the interesting bit. The owner is now going to present their logistical solution. As he is talking through, I keep wondering whether they have actually read the specification that we have sent as part of the RFP process. We clearly stated the importance of seasonality of our products. It seems they are working with averages only. Not sure their solution is going to work out.

We are sitting through the 76 slides which has consumed about 110 minutes in total which means we have 10 minutes left for questions and closing. At this stage, the owner has been the one doing all the talking. I couldn't help but notice that the operational manager hesitated to jump in when the owner was saying something which he clearly didn't agree to. It can be such a blessing watching body language.

Unfortunately, 10 minutes is not enough to answer all the questions we have so we are going to focus on the ones that are most important. Our logistics manager asks if they have taken the seasonality of our products into consideration at which point the owner and operational manage look at each other in disbelief and then start to dig through some documents that they have brought with them. They state that they will look into this and come back to us at a later stage.

When time is up, we thank them for their visit and as they leave, I'm thinking: "only" 3 more suppliers left for the day.

Lessons learned

Beforehand:
- Give the buyer and logistics manager a call prior to meeting. Research has shown that establishing contact before a meeting will improve the outcome of the meeting itself.
- During this conversation, ask what the 3-5 top things are that you need to consider for your response. What are their key priorities? Don't assume. Ask.
- Ask how they consider the best use of the 2 hours we have together. Of course, feel free to make your own suggestion if asked. I would suggest 30 minutes introduction, 30 minutes clarifying your assumption, 30 minutes presenting your solution and 30 minutes for questions and next steps.
- Decide who will be present. Don't just fill the room with people who have nothing to add. If you're that inefficient with people's time, how can you run an efficient operation? I already assume it's going to be overstaffed. The people in the room need to have something to say or else they shouldn't join in.
- Agree internally on roles and responsibilities by making sure you know who will do or say what during the meeting.

During:
- Arrive on time for meetings. It's better to be 30 mins early than 3 minutes late.
- Make sure your laptop is working properly. How will you run a multi-million business if you don't even have your own equipment in order?
- You have two ears and one mouth. That's exactly the listening vs talking ratio.
- Don't sell your solution. Sell the solution that the customer needs.
- Make sure you write down the questions asked so you can build that into your next proposal.
- Agree on a follow-up process. Clarify if the timings in the RFP process are still accurate.

After:
- Do as you promise. Follow through on the questions asked with an e-mail containing your proposal and any additional information requested.
- Ensure you stick to the timelines as stated in the communication process.

So, there it is, just another day in the real life of a procurement manager. Did you recognise yourself anywhere in there? Please think about us; about our goals and challenges, what we want, what our priorities are. If you do that, your chance of success is much greater.

Having spent 17 years at Mars, with 15 years in various procurement roles, **Mark Schenkius** set up his own company in 2018. He provides training and consultancy to sales professionals. Having had experience in all aspects of procurement he really does have some unique insights into the mind of a buyer. He uses this knowledge to train sales professionals to become better negotiators and to take a more strategic approach to their buying counterparts.

He is also the author of "The Other Side of Sales" where he shares many secrets of dealing with professional buyers.

If you'd like to find out what he can do to help you, please do not hesitate to check out his website **www.roi-10.com**, reach out to him via **Linkedin** or email at: **mark@roi-10.com**

Notes

35 | Lateral Thinking in Gritty Negotiations

By Patrick Tinney

"In business and in life, you don't get what you deserve, you get what you negotiate."

Chester L Karrass

Rather than talking about some negotiation theory, I decided to share a real-world story from the hard front-line of negotiation in this chapter. This story will form part of my fourth book, due out in 2022.

When I was in my 20's and working at The Oakville Journal Record (OJR), selling advertising space, I discovered my first business mentor. His name is Bobby Hillier. Bob is about 15 years older than me and had been trained in the crusty old school Thomson Newspaper culture. Bob would sit me down at lunch or over "a pop" (code for beer) after work and tell me about his newspaper history, the history of the business and how to be successful.

Bob had all of these cool ways of selling. He was always a pro's pro and understood that the last part of any sale is actually getting paid. I cannot tell you how many scammers we ran into in those days, who thought they could just run up big bills and then not pay up. The problem for sales professionals such as Bob and I who sold on commission is that, if the customer did not pay their bills, our credit department would just claw our commissions back. This is why Bob would get into my head about the practice that qualifying customers who paid, was almost as important as selling. This is precisely why in my own sales and negotiation learning practice; I qualify all who I work with. I cannot tell you what lengths I will go to, so that I can understand a customer's culture and payment history. This extra step saves so much time and money. Today, in the midst of a pandemic your time is so precious. You cannot waste it.

Now back to the OJR. It was a beautiful summer day, just before lunch. Bob walked by my desk and said *"Paddy... grab a pad of lined paper and slap it on a clip board and grab a pen. You and I are off to make a call."* Bob does everything fast. So, we beetle down the front stairs of the newspaper and started walking east up Lakeshore Road in Oakville. Bob said *"Pat this is going to be a tough call.*

Here is what I want you to do. We are going to enter the stereo store at the end of the block, and I want you to separate from me immediately once we get into the store. I am going to have a conversation with the store owner. Do not speak to me or the owner. Once we get into the store, I want you to walk over to the highest end stereo equipment the store owner sells. I want you to write down the names, serial numbers and prices of about 15 pieces of equipment. Pat, I want you to have a totally straight face. Be expressionless. Do this quickly like you have done this before. Then exit the store without looking at me or the owner and wait for me outside. Got it?" I said *"Got it!"*

Bob emerged from the store a few minutes later and walked very quickly back to the OJR with me in tow. I said *"Bob what was that all about? What were you doing and what was I doing?"* He said *"Pat, the guy in the stereo store is leaking into 45 days and he owes us a pile of money for all of the ads we have run for him. I know he is getting some Co-op dollars, so there is money coming in. Our credit ladies at the back of the office told me that if I don't come up with a big check to clear his account, they will dock my commission and they might even roll some of my pay back. Today, was the day that I had to tell the stereo owner that he had 48 hours to pay up or there would be consequences."* We walked a little further back to the office, and I asked Bob *"So why did you have me along on this call and what was with the clip board and all of the taking stock?"* Bob replied *"When we went into the store I walked up to the front desk and greeted the store manager and said I had tough news. With your back pointed to me, I whispered to the store owner that the young guy with me is from our credit department. I am under a lot of pressure to clear your account. The guys in credit are not happy and sent this guy with me to understand how much inventory you have; in case we have to take action."* Bob said *"I told him, I don't like this any more than you, but we ran your ads in good faith and now I need a check in 48 hours. I will see you in two days."*

Two days later Bob got a check from the stereo store owner. The credit folks were happy. The account was up to date and Bob announced that he was leaving the newspaper to go work out in Edmonton at The Edmonton Sun.

That week the newspaper gave Bob a great send off. There was a real party atmosphere. There were thank you speeches and we gave Bob a car-heater as a goodbye gift. Edmonton winters in those days were epic owing to the sustained stretches of arctic air that would sweep into Edmonton and just stay there for weeks on end. Bob loved his gifts. We took pictures. Bob left with all of his accounts cleaned up.

On Monday, I get called into the advertising manager's office. He said *"Pat, until we hire a replacement for Bob we are splitting up his accounts, so there are no gaps with our customers."* With that he handed me a list. It was about 10 accounts long and the bottom account was....the stereo store!!! I stared at the list and left the office without a word. There was no negotiation with the business when the OJR was short-handed.

After a couple of days, I decided to call on the stereo store to fill the owner in on Bob's departure and my new responsibilities with his account. I waited until his store was empty and I walked in. The owner was behind the counter and as soon as he saw me, he had this "what does this guy want?" look! I said, *"Good morning. Bob has moved to Edmonton, and I will be servicing your account until we hire a new sales person. How can I help you this week on behalf of the OJR? What models are selling best right now, and may I draft up some new creative ideas and show them to you?"* Then I stopped speaking and just stared at him. There was an awful silence for the longest time. As the store owner was processing what I had just shared with him, his face twisted and distorted in about three different directions at once. He looked like a guy chewing on an angry wasp. True story. #Giddyup #Youcantstopme.

Lessons Learned. All too often we think of a negotiation as a linear process. You speak, they speak. The lesson I learned from this situation is that there are non-verbal ways to position yourself, other things you can do, steps you can take, to help build and defend your position. In this case we used a strategy tied to a set of almost theatrical tactics. It was not pretty but it served its purpose. We were paid for services rendered.

Patrick Tinney is the Founder and Managing Partner of Centroid Training and Marketing and author of three sales books "Perpetual Hunger: Sales Prospecting Lessons & Strategy" and "Unlocking Yes the Revised Edition: Sales Negotiation Lessons & Strategy" and "The Bonus Round: Corporate Sales Lessons & Strategy". Prior to Centroid, Patrick held various corporate sales and management positions at The Toronto Star, The Southam Newspaper Group, Hollinger Inc. and CanWest Media.

Over his 40-year career Patrick has concluded multi-million dollar media sales and negotiation solutions for many of Canada's largest advertisers. An expert on the topics of sales prospecting, consultative selling and sales negotiation, Patrick is a frequent sales podcast guest, and is published in online and print business journals.

www.centroidmarketing.com

Notes

36

Adding Value Outside of Your Own Sale

By Jim Irving

"If it doesn't add value, it's waste."

Henry Ford

Everyone has their own definition of value. Some think it means 'cheap'. It doesn't. Some think you can't define it. You usually can. Some think it's only about a monetary number. It's far broader than that.

Put in the simplest way possible, you could say this –

Your investment – the cost = value

But that cost of investment could be money, or future money, or time or effort or disruption, or any combination of these. Those from the procurement or finance side of businesses also measure the value of money using tools so they can compare different prospective investments better. Things like ROI, IRR, and Opportunity Cost. I am not going to go through these definitions in detail here, but if you don't know what these are and you are selling complex and/or expensive B2B solutions, you really need to.

Opportunity Cost is interesting. It is best defined as *"the cost in terms of foregoing alternatives".* What does this mean? If you are the customer and you have money to invest in just one project, and say, three different projects that you could invest in. You can look at each by their Return on Investment (ROI), Internal Rate of Return (IRR) and, perhaps most importantly by the opportunity cost. What don't you get if you put all the money into one of these projects? Do you lose more than you could gain? This is the underlying cause of many of those *"I have no idea how I lost that deal"* conversations back at the office. The project that was funded was perhaps even nothing at all to do with your area of the business – the worst case of the 'unknown competitor'.

But the investment in the above simple equation, isn't always a financial one. If you are really tight on resource, then the same calculation has to be made in terms of allocating people and resources. It can be, and often is, much more than just 'the money'. And the value delivered can also be non-financial too – improved service levels, improved corporate image, happier staff, reduced business risk etc.

So, we have now looked at the concept of value in business. It's absolutely core to any sale. People and organisations buy only because they can see value in doing so. Trust me, none of your prospects wake up in the morning, get to the office and think to themselves *"Oh, I really want to buy a (insert your product or service here) today"! BUT, they may well be thinking "I wish there was a way to improve this situation", or, "how can we gain competitive advantage here?"*. Then, if you deliver value to support them with their challenges, objectives, and issues, you can deliver value to them.

Your prospects are never interested in your company, and particularly your history (how many presentations start with that!). They could very well be interested in what you can do to help them. Always think of outcomes, not your products or services. What do they deliver to the prospect?

Two tips on this aspect of selling –

1. Look at your messaging. Listen to yourself as you speak. Look back at the emails you have sent out. Look at your website. Are they talking about your offerings, or what those offerings deliver? The simplest way to make a positive change is 'WMT', 'Which Means That'. *"Our product is 10% faster than the competition".* Not good, far better would be *"Our product is 10% faster than the competition, which means that you can get your goods to market 3 days quicker".* Or *"this leads to" or "this means" or "so" or "allowing you to".* All of these change your message from a product one to a much stronger and meaningful outcome based one to your prospect. It is now based on their results and potential.

2. Another approach which has also been around for many years is this. Instead of always thinking and saying, *"This is what our product does"*, try to think instead in terms of *"This is what you can do with our product/service"*. Do you see that difference? It's now pointing to them and their world and challenges, not to your product features.

All the above comments are by way of the longest introduction I have ever made to a subject! In fact, it's longer than the subject will be! Because the title of the chapter is *"Add value outside of your own sale"* not value itself. However, it was important, as you need to better understand value before you can move to the real chapter subject!

If you sell in volume and have no need for any form of relationship of any kind, what follows isn't for you. But for the vast majority of salespeople this can add enormous competitive advantage to what you do. Oh, and if you want the easiest, and laziest life possible, it is again not for you. But if you want the most profitable possible life, then please read on...

You are working with prospects, or as an account manager, in an ongoing relationship with your customer. How can you really differentiate yourself from your competitors?

Obviously, you need to know about them, ask questions and listen. But, assuming there's a good solution fit, what else can you do to help build and strengthen your new relationship? Providing great service is important, but that's another subject.

One thing I have been doing for many years now (see The B2B Selling Guidebook) is genuinely trying to add value 'outside the sale'. Assuming you know the market/ industry you are operating in, and you understand their business problems (even – and especially – those not directly related to your solution), ask yourself *"what have I read, what examples have I seen of similar companies doing something clever, fixing their challenges etc?".* Pass those on to your prospect/customer in conversation or as a 'by the way' addition to emails. What you are now doing is adding value outside of your own sale. Companies tend to like salespeople who deliver value to them. BUT they like those who also add even more value on top much, much more. What have you learned from other customers, from industry journals, from following what's happening (do look at Google Alerts – perfect for doing this with no work on your part) that you can share with your prospect/customer? You are becoming a source of advice, of useful ideas, of help and support, over and above adding simple value. Doing this will serve to separate you from around 99% of salespeople. You are not just delivering value; you are also adding 'Value+'.

The lesson. Introducing good ideas and constantly reminding them of your personal value - outside your own sale - really makes a difference to the relationship and ultimately to your revenues. More important, it makes you a better, more rounded, trusted advisor.

Notes

_____

_____

_____

_____

_____

_____

_____

_____

_____

_____

_____

_____

_____

_____

_____

_____

_____

_____

_____

_____

_____

_____

_____

_____

Appendix

Some additional reading

In the process of writing their chapters many of my guest authors mentioned sources, interesting books, and places to find out more.

Two authors further added in a series of footnotes which I felt were worth including as an appendix. Here are their 'suggested reading' lists –

Chapter 23 – Jeremy Jacobs (Lazy Pigeons)

Kahneman, D., & Tversky, A. (1982). The psychology of preference, *Scientific American, 246,* 160-173.

Nebel, J. M. (2015). Status quo bias, rationality, and conservatism about value, *Ethics, 125*(2), 449-476.

Samuelson, W., & Zeckhauser, R. J. (1988). Status quo bias in decision making, *Journal of Risk and Uncertainty, 1,* 7-59.

Kahneman D., (2011) Thinking, Fast and Slow, Penguin Books – *Random House*

Chataway R., (2020). The Behaviour Business, *Harriman House*

Shotton R., (2018). The Choice Factory, *Harriman House*

Ariely D., (2019). Predictably Irrational, *Harper*

Thaler R., & Sunstein C., (2021) Nudge – The Final Edition, *Allen Lane*

Chapter 29 – Jamie Martin (The Psychology of Selling)

C.P. Russell (1921). *How to Write a Sales-Making Letter:* Printers Ink

Dale E. Audio-visual Methods in Teaching. New York: Holt, Reinhart & Winston; 1946. Google Scholar

Mehrabian, A., & Ferris, S. R. (1967). Inference of attitudes from nonverbal communication in two channels. *Journal of Consulting Psychology, 31*(3), 248–252.

Neil A. Bradbury (216) Department of Physiology and Biophysics, Chicago Medical School, Rosalind Franklin University of Medicine and Science, North Chicago, Illinois

Purves, D., Brannon, E.M., Cabeza, R., Huettel, S.A., LaBar, K.S., Platt, M.L., & Woldorff, M.G. (2008). *Principles of Cognitive Neuroscience,* Sunderland: Sinauer Associates, Inc.

Printed in Germany
by Amazon Distribution
GmbH, Leipzig

27354495R00154